T0157507

THE NEW AGE OF
GROWING OLD

A new millennium look into age issues for the elderly, family & care givers, plus a special Section on the Dementia-Alzheimer's experience, in terms of a discussion on expanded descriptive phases of the disease

JEFFREY L. PAUL

BALBOA.
PRESS
A DIVISION OF HAY HOUSE

The information provided is not to be used as medical advice, as all questions relative to age issues and the associated issues related to age, such as various age-related diseases, thoughts or actions should all be reviewed with the appropriate medical doctor. The enclosed is more of a discussion relative to those that must deal with folks whom are aging, be it family, friends or care-givers, as not all of the items discussed are widely known, obvious, straightforward, or what might be expected. Many of the things that you will read about are not found similarly as a compilation in other books or articles on aging and the elderly. They include: retirement/assisted living care decisions & related costs, stages of care giving, falling & the reporting of falling, hospitalization documentation, Medicare information, and the multiple phases of Dementia-Alzheimer's Disease.

Balboa Press books may be ordered through booksellers or by contacting:

Balboa Press
A Division of Hay House
1663 Liberty Drive
Bloomington, IN 47403
www.balboapress.com
1 (877) 407-4847

Print information available on the last page.

ISBN: 978-1-5043-6324-2 (sc)
ISBN: 978-1-5043-6325-9 (hc)
ISBN: 978-1-5043-6357-0 (e)

Library of Congress Control Number: 2016912087

Balboa Press rev. date: 08/11/2016

THE NEW AGE OF
GROWING OLD

The following is a Family-member's Discussion, "User's" Guide, Experience and Thoughts for Dealing with Age-related Issues, Dementia-Alzheimer's, and Eventual Passing with Dignity. What Information everyone needs to know, expect, understand and plan (for) relative to their ... Aging Parents, Friends or Family.

Dedication: To my wife, mom & dad.
Special Thanks: To my sister for her contributions.

CONTENTS

Chapter 1   Introduction 1

Chapter 2   Transition Planning & Getting Ready for
                Retirement Living..5
                    •   Planning for future Medical Decisions
                    •   Advanced Directives (Planning)

Chapter 3   Getting Around in Retirement (Early &
                Later Years) 11

Chapter 4   Finances...16
                    •   Trusts

Chapter 5   Costs of Retirement Living 20

Chapter 6   Housing Decisions/Options/Transitions 23

Chapter 7   Assisted Living..32

Chapter 8   Retirement Cost Extras.....................................36

Chapter 9   Managed Care Issues & Recommendations 39

Chapter 10   Care Givers...46

Chapter 11   Elderly Health Care Issues 53

Chapter 12   Dealing with "Change" 56

Chapter 13   Mood Swings & Personality Changes 64

Chapter 14   Falling 67

Chapter 15   Hospitalization & Nursing Homes 71

Chapter 16 Medical Insurance & Prescriptions 74
Chapter 17 Medicare...78
Chapter 18 Percent of Population that is Elderly...................83
Chapter 19 Percent of Health Care Issues for the Elderly.......85
Chapter 20 Dementia – Alzheimer's 88
- When a Loved One goes through the Stages of the Disease
- Dealing with the Good Times (which are few)
- Remembering the Old Times
- Dealing with the Bad Times (most of the time)
- Forgetting what just Happened
- Coping
- Documentation & Handling of Personal Affairs of the Patient
- Help

Chapter 21 Quality of Life...97
Chapter 22 Hospice...100
Chapter 23 Passing with Dignity..102
- Care Givers
- Medical Decisions/Advanced Directives
- Living Trusts
- Final Decisions
- Funeral Arrangements

Chapter 24 The New Age of Growing Old..........................107
- Check Off Table of Key Issues

References 111

CHAPTER 1

INTRODUCTION

Healthcare is probably the most talked about issue of our time. But the discussion has not effectively included the issue of elder care and the increasing costs of this care. Please note that the information discussed herein will be relative to over 30 years of observations, opinions and information-gathering observed dealing with the elderly and final decisions related to life. This information is not contained in "how to" books. It is part of life's natural events and is due to the latest advances in medicine, health care, the costs of care, and frankly growing old now days. It is hoped that those who read this book will benefit from the information provided, as these subjects are not currently being presented in total on the news or any other outlet, and that is unfortunate. Not everyone will act the same as they reach old age, but there is knowledge to be gained by reading this book for anyone dealing with parents, friends, and neighbors that are entering these later stages of life. Knowing what my family went through (and my observations of others) with these elder care issues, many people had asked about the topics described in this book, and that was my reason for writing about it. Knowing, experiencing and dealing with the age issues and investigating the care options, costs and necessary decisions related to these issues is the foundation of this work.

Our current culture is such that it does not help one understand the issues relating to growing old. This book will focus on individual(s) during each of these later stages of life (primarily ages 65-90).

Some cultures support and honor this period of life, our current culture does not, and I believe that eventually there will be a day of reckoning, where all the sudden ramifications of aging will be a serious issue to be resolved. Let's hope that it is not too late, before that is understood. I have sat with many an elderly person waiting and waiting for their children to come by for a visit. For the children, all too often, it is, "let's put them in a home, or it's now your turn (one of the other children/family member) to take care of them". With all due respect for the families, it is currently understood that these issues are difficult. The time that must be <u>dedicated</u> to take care of elder parents, family or friends is nearly a full time job, and often takes a great toll on the health of the family member or friend whom is the Care Giver. Even if a professional Care Giver is brought in to augment the care, still family or friends must monitor the situation, including the medicines, finances, and the level of care needed.

Elder care will turn into a significant issue within the next decade, if not sooner, due to the factors of costs and availability for elder care that will continue to not meet the demand, resulting in higher costs and less availability for the average individual(s) reaching retirement age. According to the information stated from the U. S. Census Bureau[5] within the next thirty five years, by the year 2050, the population aged 65 and over is projected to be 83.7 million, nearly double what it is today. Currently there are barely adequate numbers of retirement facilities available (nearly every facility has a short waiting list), but that will not be the case in the future, when the number of facilities will not nearly meet the needs of an aging population, resulting in long waiting lists. Then what? Where will the elderly go to get proper care? The cost of elder care is skyrocketing, how will everyone be able to afford it in the future, and will there be enough Care Givers around to take care of this ever increasing age group? What about the expenses of elder care, will everyone be able to afford it? Will the state or federal government handle the costs? (Not likely!) What about those who become 65 years old with little or no savings for these care costs, or no family to help with decisions and/or the monies necessary to be able to receive the bare necessities of this care? The decisions related to medicines alone, even with an extremely competent & dedicated doctor, require someone (recommended) other than the elderly patient to successfully monitor and insure compliance (it can be done by some individuals, but a greater chance of success is if a Care Giver or family member is able to help). Without the support of friends or family, will the state or federal government be able to help them? (Again, not likely!) These questions remain unanswered and there is little consideration for the future in regards of how to deal with this <u>enormous</u> problem. The baby boomers are reaching a crossroads age of 65, how will they deal with these issues when the lack of planning has resulted in inadequate number of retirement/assisted living facilities, the needs for suitable Care Givers, and (of course) the money to pay for this care? This is another reason why this book is written – no one seems to be addressing or discussing these issues. And to make matters of greater concern, note that according to "DiscoverTheOdds.com"[12], according to the 2010 U.S. Census Report, there were 53,364 Centenarians, or 1.73 per 10,000 people in the total population (have reached age 100). Should there be some planning for a retirement that may last from age 65 to 100 (and each year the odds are better for living longer)? Having to afford 35 years of retirement living would certainly be a tremendous drain on most retirement budgets, and will there be "quality of life" living to the age of 100. What happens if the retirement funds run out?

Each Chapter will deal with the pressing issues of growing old, planning for retirement, living in retirement, and dealing with the issues of finances, health (including a special section on Dementia-Alzheimer's), the quality of life in old age, and then passing with dignity. The chapters will discuss the issues, have recommendations, options for consideration, and discuss the struggles and decisions of old age. Knowing what to expect will be a help to family, friends and Care Givers. Of course, not everyone will experience the same issues, but many will experience similar issues. For example, not every family will deal with someone that has Dementia-Alzheimer's, but there may be other health issues that will likely be dealt with at some later stage of life. The care may not be the same, but the focus of the care should be similar, with the focus on doing the best to insure continued "quality of life".

In all cases relative to health considerations & issues, a review by a doctor is recommended.

CHAPTER 2

TRANSITION PLANNING & GETTING READY FOR RETIREMENT LIVING

In a discussion of planning for the issues relative to the later years of life or old age, one must start at a transition point. For many it is when individuals reach their 50's & 60's. In the past, many believed that working hard to get ahead was a primary goal, as was providing for their family. They also believed that they should save their money for that proverbial "rainy day". That was their focus and that is what they strived for. Not sure that everyone now days has this same focus or even able to save money, due to difficult economic times and that may lead to significant problems in the future. Will everyone be able to retire with savings, pensions, health care benefits/insurance, Medicare and Social Security to meet their needs? It may have been the "normal" for the elderly of the American Family of the 1980's, but not the "norm" now days.

Some may consider early retirement when they reach their 50's & 60's. This decision is an important one, and requires considerable planning, both from a financial standpoint and also a health standpoint. Many have made the wrong decision here. There are many stories of those that retired early and planned for various scenarios, travel, etc. only to find that they are unhappy and unfulfilled, which can lead to some serious consequences, especially from a health standpoint. Working may have kept them going; stop working may result in degradation in health. The lesson to be learned is that planning for one's retirement is very important, and staying busy should be part of that plan. It may mean taking up a hobby, volunteering, going to school, or working part-time, etc. If health issues of magnitude occur, nothing else controls the status of this transitional period with associated expenses, except health.

Planning for future Medical Decisions

A health issue could now change everything and especially the roles for people's lives. If one of the spouse's has a health issue, it is typical (if physically possible) that the other spouse becomes the "Care Giver". If not the other spouse, then the responsibility for care falls to the family, children or friends. If not living close by, the children or family may have difficulty in assisting with this care (the amount of time for this care may be substantial). The amount of care necessary may be equivalent to a full time job, especially if the Care Giver (child or family member) does not live with the parent. The family Care Giver should expect, even during this early transitional period of receiving phones calls at all times, even late in the night or early morning, on health issues, or the worst scenario – falling (reference Chapter 14).

In the past, many people were often able to retire with a proper "nest egg" to meet most of their financial and health care costs for a planned 10 or 20 year period (what will happen in the future, as medical advances are resulting in the potential for a 30 to 40 year retirement period?). If retirement comes a little earlier than expected, this adds an unplanned burden for the family. Now, if not financially set, will the costs (a portion) of elder care get to be the responsibility of the family/children (or the government?). Neither is a very good option, nor something that either the family/children or the government are planning to cover.

Of course during this transitional period, health issues may start to occur at a more frequent rate, which could eat into some of the savings that may have been planned for retirement. Even with health care insurance plans or Medicare, often not all the costs are covered. Certainly heart related diseases are more prevalent starting in the 50's & 60's, as is cancer, diabetes, etc. (reference Chapter 19, which will list the percentages of health care issues for the elderly). Many health care issues may be a function of a lifestyle that can no longer be tolerated without consequences (smoking, stress, bad eating habits, etc.). Other common age-related issues may affect the body such as: back pain, hip and knee issues, etc. Even if surgeries are required and are successful, and perhaps paid for primarily by health care insurance plans, that will not cover all the costs of now required prescriptions that one may require for the rest of their lives. The prescription costs will be a potentially substantial part of the future of one's personal budget from now on, again, cutting into the (savings) monies that may have been set aside for retirement. Sure the prescriptions may be paid for (primarily) by the health care insurance, but the co-pays can still result in significant costs for the retired individual that is on a fixed income.

Consideration for Retirement Planning should begin in life as early as possible. Realistically, it is likely to start when people reach their 30's or 40's. Hopefully, there has been an opportunity in life to accumulate savings, such as an accumulation of monies in a 401K Savings Plan that can be used to cover retirement costs. Perhaps equity in a home will be able to be used to cover future retirement costs. Or, maybe a combination of both will be used for retirement. Thus, it is important to start thinking about financial planning for the future as early in life as possible.

Advanced Directives (Planning)

Financial Planning is so important, and this also means looking into the planning relative to Trusts and Wills (reference Chapter 4). They will document how Financial and Healthcare Decisions are made if the individuals are no longer mentally competent to make such decisions. "Advanced Healthcare Directives" (as listed in the Trust Documents) are certainly an important document that everyone should have developed and (especially) available (to present to health care providers/hospitals) at all times. Templates for estate planning and trust documents are easily found on the Internet, but it is strongly recommended that the finalized documents be reviewed with a trust lawyer (or perhaps the trust lawyer will formulate the documents). Now days, nearly every time an adult goes to a Hospital, the Hospital will ask for a copy of one's Healthcare Directives. It is extremely important that families start the discussions about these Financial and Healthcare Decisions while the individual is still mentally competent. Emotions and family arguments can be extremely difficult if these decisions are not discussed before an emergency or one is no longer mentally competent. In the Trust Documents, there will be established an order as to whom is first (often referred to as the Successor Trustee), second (Trustee) & third (Trustee) in line to make the critical decisions for the family member. If the family member is no longer competent, the individual that is designated first in line has the critical decision making ability that could affect the very life of the family member. Thus, the one listed in the Trust Documents, as "first in line" to make decisions should be aware of the wishes of the family member that (now) is no longer capable of making their own perhaps critical life and death decision. This is why it is so critical to discuss these decisions while the family/individual is still able to share their wishes, as it tends to get much more difficult later.

Taking the reins of these health care decisions can be difficult if the individual is still alive, yet cognizant enough to think that they are not mentally incompetent. Generally in order to prove that the individual is mentally incompetent, what needs to occur is that the family member must have doctors (3) sign affidavits that the individual is not mentally capable of handling their own decisions, in order for the "first in line" family member to now be in charge of all financial and health care decisions. This becomes a significant family emotional issue. For the family member that is now incompetent, this procedure is the most effective. This scenario has already been agreed upon by the family member whom already has agreed to the transfer of decisions, as laid out in their Trust Document's Healthcare/Financial Directives.

Essential family transitional planning should include having a current list of all medicines that the individual's are taking. Any special dietary information should also be part of the list in case there is an overnight stay (at a hospital). Additionally, either copies or (now) having a card that lists the Advanced Health Care Directive, which includes such information (from the Trust Documents) as to whom can make the medical decisions if the individual is incapacitated, is very important. Perhaps the local Hospital can be given a copy of this information prior to the inevitable occurrence of a future visit. The (Trust's) Health Care Directive will also list information on whether or not to resuscitate in the unfortunate instance of a life threatening situation. Does the individual want to be kept alive by machines? Who will make these difficult decisions? These are issues that are extremely emotional and should be discussed and documented before the fact. Of course, this does not ease the emotional heartache that occurs at these very difficult times for the Family.

The above issues are all part of the transitional planning and getting ready for the retirement years. Perhaps it seems to be too early in the Retirement Years to think about health care and associated cost decisions; however, the need to be ready for these decisions is best, if planned well in advance. Then, when the unthinkable happens everyone is prepared. With the potential for mental health issues to hasten the takeover of the health/ financial decisions (by the children, or family, as trustees), these can be stressful times for all involved. With the Trusts/Directives and Wills in place, the stress is reduced for everyone and retirement can be enjoyed to greatest extent possible. Transitioning into retirement living is a major milestone in life. Health care and living residence location, along with the associated costs are now prime concerns. Equally important is to have the proper legal documents developed and available.

CHAPTER 3

GETTING AROUND IN RETIREMENT (EARLY & LATER YEARS)

Getting around, travelling, etc. is generally not an issue during the early retirement years, ages 50's & 60's. Because of this, it is best to take advantage of the ability to easily get around (physically) and travel, because it will not be long before this may no longer the case, when reaching ages 70's & 80's, no matter that the monies may be available for travel in these later years. Typically, during the retirement years, the trips and travel activities are closer to home, perhaps due to the need for specific requirements, often related to health issues. Eating out may tend to be at the familiar places, i.e. the same restaurants, many times over.

In the event of significant health issues during the ages 50's & 60's, getting around could also be difficult for some. Travel for even the normal human necessities can be a struggle. Travel of even short distances to go get groceries or prescriptions must be a task planned in advance of the needs. Fortunately, now days there are both grocery stores and pharmacies that will deliver. Deliveries can be ordered on the internet or called in over the phone. This is another cost (deliveries) that adds to the costs of (retirement) living in this transitional period of life. Not many will plan for this scenario either. Of course, not all communities have these delivery services, thus, this becomes a decision (the need to have necessities readily available) during the transition: the need to move from the "family" home to a retirement facility, even prior to the decision about moving into assisted care or a retirement/nursing home facility, which will likely be a decision later, and require total dependence on others for transportation.

The ability to drive and travel becomes less and less viable. The ability to visit family or friends becomes more difficult. Driving and traveling late is tiresome and means more stress on the elderly, thus they tend to stay closer to their home. This is a mixed blessing, as the ability to drive a car should be a consideration (by the family, others) as to whether the folks once they reach this age are really safe in the operation of a motor vehicle. Society should consider this also, and rather than giving older folks their licenses (regularly) just because they may not have accidents, a better policy would be that when one reaches 75 years of age, they should be tested in a motor vehicle every two years. This would save lives and reduce accidents. The issue is that as one ages, their reflexes affect their capability for safe driving. Other critical considerations for the elderly being able to drive are eyesight and hearing. A renewal driver's license is sent in the mail (California), if there are no recent accidents or incidents (ticket). This policy needs to change.

Eventually it is realized that it is no longer safe to drive a motor vehicle at this age (typically when one reaches their 80's). Hopefully this decision is made before any one gets hurt. Any time that individuals of this age do go into the DMV for a renewal, usually, they are not renewed. It does not take long for the examiner to determine that the elderly person should no longer be driving. Note, that even without the capability to drive, an equivalent of a license can still be obtained for identification.

Without the ability to drive any longer, most elderly folks hope that family come to visit them (more often than before, and this is an opportunity to go to the grocery or drug store). However, due to the busy schedules of the family, there may not be time for this local travel. The elderly are frustrated by this situation. For individuals living by themselves either in a retirement/assisted living facility, or at home, this results in a feeling of loneliness.

As people reach their eighties (80's), getting around is even more of an issue. Whether it is getting around their surroundings (family home or retirement facility) or traveling or driving (if still able to do so), decisions and options for getting around have reached an important aspect of their lives. In terms of getting around their immediate surroundings, the physical nature of movement is more difficult, and thus assistance is now a likely requirement, be it a cane, walker or wheel chair, etc. This certainly results in a change of the life style. Though movement is more difficult, it is recommended that physical movement continue as much as possible, as directed/approved by a doctor. Getting physical exercise, i.e. walking, or stretching is very important and helps to reduce the chance of further, unpleasant physical limitations, and certainly the chance of falling, which is now a considerable risk. Getting around with a cane or walker could be a new activity, but it should be supervised by a knowledgeable Care Giver or Nurse. If not maintaining the proper posture, this could result in further physical degradation and serious medical issues related to the back and knees, primarily.

At this stage in life, people may have a difficult time adjusting to this more sedimentary life style. Certainly, if still capable, getting around or traveling even short distances is recommended. There will eventually reach a time when even short travel will not be feasible. Thus, the Retirement Facility Apartment or Family

Home becomes the only world that is known. Eventually, walkers or wheel chairs may be the only way the Folks have to be able to get around at all (unfortunately).

Most retirement/assisted living facilities have vans or small buses in order to transport folks from place to place, especially to doctor's appointments. These vans are also used to transport the folks to various activities, i.e. visiting the local grocery store, or perhaps special events, like travel to a museum, park or even a gambling casino. It is recommended that the retirees get used to this mode of transportation, especially if they need assistance in getting around (as mentioned with a walker or wheel chair), as most of these retirement facility vehicles have wheel chair lifts. The retirement facilities will have a weekly activities list showing where the vans/buses will be traveling for that week. The vehicles are generally considered as part of the costs of the retirement facility; only a special use may require an additional fee to be paid to the facility. The use of these vehicles or their costs and availability should be something that is reviewed prior to moving into the retirement/assisted living facility.

If a family car is to be kept at the retirement/assisted living facility, most have limited parking available, thus a decision should be made if it is necessary to continue to keep a family vehicle, as parking fees could add up, and if no longer used, these costs may not make financial sense. Of course, this is a significant "change" and may result in stress and heartache (giving up the car even if it is no longer being used), and thus the family should tread lightly here. Eventually, the obvious non-use of the family vehicle may make this decision easier to accept (its sell or removal), especially if the parking or insurance bills keeping adding up in the budget (as an addition to the retirement/assisted care facility) expenses. Without the availability of a vehicle, now the resident retirees must rely primarily on the retirement facility (van) for the majority of transportation, i.e., doctor visits.

In the retirement years, getting around physically is certainly a life changing realization. Similarly, travel by vehicle means primarily relying on others (be it a retirement home van, of a Care Giver providing that transportation).

CHAPTER 4

FINANCES

Financial planning for retirement and the certainty of old age scenarios should start as early in life as possible. It is critical that individuals start thinking about it directly, if they have reached their 40's, 50's or 60's. If savings or monies have not been set aside yet, it is time to set some aside or come up with a plan of how things can be handled in the inevitability, which is growing old and being able to handle the circumstances related to living comfortably in the later (retirement) years of life. During this transitional period, a review of finances/investments is probably the most critical as of any time in one's life. This can be done with professional finance experts, preferably with the family in attendance. Now days, there are so many considerations and options, a review with certified financial planners may be the best option and financial decision.

Not having the "nest egg" of monies set aside for retirement and old age situations is not necessarily "a show stopper". There are options available, for those that may own a home, for example, the possibility of a "reverse mortgage". The reverse mortgage may be able to provide some of the funds necessary for retirement. Considerations of retirement homes/assisted living options; or even (remodeling/modifications) to an existing home that would allow for better elder living conditions; making bathrooms, kitchens, etc. more "age friendly" and safer, are so important.

By this stage of life, there are only a few options left to change one's financial status. If still living in the family home, there is the option to sell it, and then go to a retirement/assisted living facility. The proceeds of the sale (the equity) would certainly add to the amount of monies available, needed now for retirement health care and living issues. This decision certainly changes the decision relative to living out their lives at home. The option of a reverse mortgage, using the equity in the family home, meeting the criteria of being older than 62 years of age, would assist with the funds for health care and retirement living costs. An option for monies resulting from the reverse mortgage monies is to upgrade the home for the folks, making it safer and efficient relative to being age-friendly. Or, perhaps this money could be used for required additional care-givers that come into the home. But everyone should look at the merits, advantages and disadvantages of a reverse mortgage. The reverse mortgage could result in additional monies, but could affect family considerations of inheritance monies by the children. Another option might be to just take a "traditional" loan out against the home (for example an equity line of credit), again, if the equity is available. The best answer is to review the situation with an unbiased (if possible) financial advisor, one that does not have a stake in either financial option. Other than equity in a home, there are few options left to raise monies for health care and living expenses at this stage of life. One recent option that is just beginning to become more popular (while still working) is to set aside monies for retirement living (much as one might set aside monies for a 401K). However, it is likely that only a very small percentage of the population is considering and actually setting aside these monies (or can afford to do so).

There are some additional supplemental financial options available for some individuals. If a former military member, there are programs available to help augment retirement home costs. This may be dependent on the financial status of the retiree. A review of the financial situation will be necessary to determine how much money may be available to augment current available monies, savings, etc. Other funds may be added for retirement; perhaps there are valuables that could be sold, i.e. furniture, jewelry, stocks, and bonds. This may seem somewhat of a last resort, but if one's health care is at stake, these become important, yet unpleasant decisions to be made.

When individuals finally reach retirement age, everything now tends to revolve around the finances; to insure that the existing funds are adequate now and especially for the future. For Savings Accounts (to be used later in retirement), decisions need to be discussed with financial experts (recommended) to review the strategies for these accounts. Should the accounts be more conservative to make the funds more liquid (more available now or in the future)? These are important decisions, and likely every situation will be different. The important things are the considerations of retirement costs now and any adjustments for the future. Certainly, staying in the family home or moving to a retirement facility (with monthly rental payments) are critical financial decisions.

Trusts

As noted, Trusts are important documents for the Family. Trusts can protect the family's interests now and in the future. The language for the Trust should be discussed with a Trust Lawyer. The Trust documents are important for dealing with the financial decisions, medical decisions and the inevitably that comes with one's passing and their associated wishes. Living

Trusts should lay out the requests, the needs and the wishes of the retired individuals.

Along with the health issues, the finances are the biggest concern for the Retirees and their Family. It is so important that the finances (monies) are available to cover the full retirement costs and expenses (which now days may mean 30 or 40 years). This is not an easy situation and may require constant monitoring or review to insure the best results and money is available until the inevitable passing.

CHAPTER 5

COSTS OF RETIREMENT LIVING

The costs associated with retirement should be reviewed and planned as soon as possible. This should be done prior to retirement, in order to reduce the stress of this issue once retirement age has been reached. In retirement planning, one needs to get an accurate number on monthly living expenses. The best way to do this is to figure out your fixed monthly expenses. Next, compute your average monthly expenses (which may include some variable items that occur from time to time)."[10] Certainly health care costs play a significant role in determination of these costs. Thus, all potential expenses in a worst case scenario of the costs need to assume some potential or even routine health issues, based upon known health issues or health issues that may occur in the family (historically), such as a history of heart disease.

"Among older Americans, average annual expenditures peaked at about $61,000 for those in the 45-54 year age range, according to data (2014) from the Consumer Expenditures Survey. By ages 55-64, spending dipped to $56,000, and down again to $46,000 between ages 65 to 74. At 75 years and older, average spending was only $34,000, though health care expenses may spike up for many." That is the great concern: what happens to these spending amounts when all of the sudden, a move to a retirement/assisted living facility may require as much as $100,000 per year or more for the housing, managed care (medicines), care givers and extra care for additional health issues, as noted below?

Now days "in the U.S., Medicare does not cover the costs of independent or dependent care. Some long term insurance plans with home care benefits may contribute to independent or dependent living expenses. For most people, though, the expenses will have to be covered by pensions, savings, or the sale of a home or other assets"[10]

The expenses related to living into retirement can be considerable, and certainly more than planned (no one can anticipate major health issues that come with age), and result in further unplanned expenses. The majority of the expenses at this stage of life will be: (1) Retirement/Assisted Living Facility or Family Home Costs; (2) Retirement/Assisted Living Facility, where there may be a need for augmented Care Givers (more than the staff of the facility) due to health and/or physical limitations or considerations; (3) Retirement/Assisted Living Facility, that results in each resident being evaluated on the level of Care that they will need, certainly those requiring more services will pay more for their care (4) Additional costs for Care for food service, if delivered at the Family Home, or delivered from a Dining Area of the Retirement Facility (if the individuals are physically incapable of going to the Dining Area, or require a tray of food brought to the room (this is an extra cost, not part of the Retirement Facility Standard Fees (which generally only consist of the apartment rental fees); (5) Prescription Drugs; and (6) General necessities: Phone, Cable Television/Internet, Miscellaneous Groceries, Clothing/Shoes & Personal Hygiene Products.

Retirement facilities' costs, for those that can afford them, are very high, often greater than $3,000-4,000/month, or $36,000-48,000/year, just for a one or two bedroom apartment. But the costs do not stop there. If one requires special care that is an additional cost. These include costs for special diets, and/or costs for more routine checks of the Residents during the day or at night, due to health concerns. There is often a weighted system of costs (based on resident specialty needs or care) that could result in another $1,000/month. But even that care may not be enough, as there may need to be in-room Care Givers that augment the Facility Staff. With the addition of Care Givers for multiple hours each day, the cost of care can add another $3,000-4,000/month. Now the costs can increase to nearly $6,000 - $8,000/month, or nearly $100,000/year. Add in the average fixed and variable expenditures, and now the spending total may be closer to $134,000 per year.

Not very many people can afford these costs as a family, and certainly not for long. But there are not many options, especially when adding expenses due to serious physical and/or mental health issues. Care for a loved one must occur, and meeting the costs of care could be difficult.

CHAPTER 6

HOUSING DECISIONS/ OPTIONS/TRANSITIONS

In retirement, a primary decision that needs to be determined is where to live. Even before retirement, this is an important consideration. The living situation may start out at one location in retirement, but due to health situations, it could change and result in the need for the individuals to move to a higher level of care assisted living situation. The retirement facilities or assisted living facilities have different levels of care depending upon the needs of the individuals. Early on, when individuals can still get around physically and mentally, the retirement facility will only need to (primarily) handle one's meals. Often large dining rooms are available for each of the residents to enjoy the company of other retirees. Additionally, activities are offered and individuals can travel to nearby community sites, museums, tourist destinations, casinos, or even a grocery or department store. Typically buses or vans are provided for this travel. These sorts of activities do tend to add some fulfillment to an otherwise (seemingly) routine living situation. Some individuals thrive in these conditions, while others resent them, and would have rather stayed in the family home. Large homes that supported the children and the family no longer make sense from an economic standpoint, i.e. why maintain extra bedrooms that no one is using, except during the sometimes rare visits of family. But the "family home" is just that, often difficult to move away from due to the memories. The family home may work out in the transitional years, however, plans to modify it to meet the challenges of old age should start right away (if planning on staying there). The longer the individuals stay in the family home, the more difficult it is for the transitional move out of it to a retirement/assisted living facility (which may have a waiting list).

Making decisions early that will have ramifications later on are very important. It is important to have a discussion with the retiree's about their housing wishes as soon as possible. Should the family home be made "age-friendly", by adding equipment, for example, in the bathrooms to reduce the risks of falls, such as railings or bars for support and balance? If multiple levels, should equipment be added to stairs for ease to transverse up and down. Perhaps the kitchen can be remodeled for ease of someone coming in to cook meals? Relative to Care Givers, can the home be modified, and perhaps spare bedrooms can be modified for "live-in" Care Givers. With the number of individuals requiring assistance in their later years in the future, and without the availability (long waiting lists) perhaps of retirement/assisted living facilities, these options may become the only viable ones. These are important decisions, and they really need to be made early, prior to retirement. Delaying these decisions will make it difficult for themselves and certainly for family.

The transitional decision to move from the Family Home into a Retirement/Assisted Living Facility (in the retirement years, after living at home successfully) is an important and difficult decision. The folks were certainly set (and likely felt that way) in their Home. But often there are factors, even for a home modified for older occupants, where worsening health; and especially mobility issues are often the resultant issue that forces a move into a Retirement/Assisted Living Facility. If the individuals are now dependent on walkers or wheel chairs, or can't get out of bed or a chair with assistance, it is likely that a move is the best answer for continued quality of life. We will discuss Quality of Life in greater detail in Chapter 21.

If deciding to stay living at the Family Home, it is recommended that Care Givers be given the responsibility for the dispensing of medicines. This will likely be an additional cost of this care, but it is a necessary one. At this age, individuals, though they may say otherwise, can be forgetful with the medicines, and there is no room for error.

Miscellaneous consumable products, groceries and personal hygiene products are a necessity. There must be a plan for the capability of getting these items and maintaining a proper stock. Can the retirees still get to the grocery store, can they call and order groceries, are there requirements for delivery; can they get on the phone or internet to request an order? Will the family be able to bring them the items from the store; will the store deliver? These are questions that need to be resolved and then followed up upon to insure that there is a process that is working. The individuals may want one of these processes, that may have worked in the past (calling for a delivery), but it may no longer be an option if the store no longer provides that service. This is an item that may result in a necessary "change" (reference Chapter 12) that may not be anticipated, and thus a back-up plan needs to be developed, in order to reduce undue stress and anxiety.

There are more issues related to the decisions to leave the family home for a retirement home/assisted living. Even if the family home has been made "age friendly" with considerations for such things as bathrooms modified with safety support handles and "grab on" bars to assistance when using the bathroom, there may reach a time when, even with the addition of Care Givers brought into the home, augmenting family care giving, that all this additional physical and personal support is not enough. The monitoring of medicines, (perhaps) the need of oxygen tanks at some point (were safety, monitoring, storage and proper use issues are critical), along with the physical requirements of Care Givers and family to transport the individuals (to and from the bathroom) may be overwhelming and may have serious consequences for the Care Givers or family members trying to help. If they require a wheel chair to move around, lifting them in and out of the wheelchair can be very dangerous for the person doing it (by not using proper lifting techniques, could result in injury to the Care Givers, family members or the individuals needing the help. If not properly trained or physically able to lift upwards to 200 pounds of deadweight, this becomes a significant problem. Even if the individual weighs less, say 120 pounds, they may not be able to help the Care Giver because they don't understand instructions, perhaps due to hearing or advanced Dementia-Alzheimer's (reference Chapter 20). Thus, family and Care Givers need to know that at some point they may not be able to singularly lift the individual, without risk of injury to themselves or the individual they are trying to help. This may become the final determining factor that requires the decision to be made to move from the family home to the retirement home/assisted living situation, where trained and often multiple personnel (staff) are available for the lifting and physical movement of the Folks.

In the situation where elderly people have decided to still live in the family home, even with contracted Care Givers providing additional assistance, which is also augmenting family assistance; all this still results in considerable efforts by family. Most people do not realize that even in this scenario, a family member who is acting as the lead coordinator of care, monitoring medicines, taking people to doctor(s), perhaps monitoring finances of the home and all the other activities associated with care is in a situation where this becomes a <u>full time job</u>. If this family member, providing care, also lives in the family home, this is a full time job. The stress involved can be substantial and eventually affect this care-giving family member. Even if this care-giving family member doesn't live in the home, but perhaps close by, it can still be a full time, stressful job that can lead to health issues for this family care giver. Some family's way of dealing with major decision making is to rotate this decision making role between family members. If the care-giving family member, any or all of them can no longer provide this function because of the stress and their own well-being, this too may force the issue of having/requiring a move into the retirement/assisted living facility. This may be an unfortunate but necessary requirement and thus finalizes the need to move into the retirement/assisted living facility and thus leave the family home once and for all.

The decision to either stay in the family home or move into a retirement/assisted living facility can have more than just financial or health issues as part of the ultimate decision. The location of the family home becomes an issue of consideration also. There may be benefits of rural living, but perhaps not in the later years of life, when necessities are farther away. There may be benefits of living in large metropolitan areas, with the advantages of more health care facilities, but there may also be more stress and pressures of this lifestyle. All these factors must be considered in the final decisions of staying at home or going to a retirement/assisted living facility. Finally, it should be realized that the living location decision could change as one's health care and needs change, thus starting out at the family home may be fine for a while, but if additional or round-the-clock care is needed, assisted living may be the final result.

Thus, what are the options, when it has been decided that the family home is no longer a viable solution for the Folks? "There are many types of independent living facilities, from apartment complexes to separate houses, which range in cost and the services provided (expect waiting lists for all):

- **Low-income or subsidized senior housing**. In the U. S there are senior housing complexes subsidized by the U.S. Department of Housing and Urban Development (HUD) for low-income seniors.
- **Senior apartments or congregate care housing**. These are apartment complexes restricted by age, usually 55 and older. Rent may include community services such as recreational programs, transportation services, and meals served in a communal dining room.
- **Retirement homes/retirement communities**. Retirement communities are groups of housing units restricted for those over a certain age, often 55 or 62 or older. These housing units can be single-family homes, duplexes, mobile homes, townhouses, or condominiums. If you decide to buy a unit, additional monthly fees may cover services such as outside maintenance, recreation centers, or clubhouses (perhaps controlled by something similar to an HOA – Home Owner's Association).
- **Continuing Care Retirement Communities (CCRCs)**. If you or your spouse are relatively healthy now, but anticipate significant health problems (later) you may want to consider at CCRC. These facilities offer a spectrum of care from independent living to nursing home care in the same community. If residents begin to need help with activities of daily living, for example, they can transfer from independent living to an assisted living or skilled

nursing facility on the same site. The main benefit of a CCRC is that you only need to relocate once to a new environment and can maintain you independence for as long as possible."[10]

For assisted living or dependent care in a retirement care facility:

- **Retirement/Assisted Care (or Nursing Home, or Residential Care Facility for the Elderly).** These facilities include complete apartment accommodations, one or two bedrooms, with a living/dining room and kitchen (no stove or cooking allowed). The facility is typically staffed round-the-clock, and the level of assistance is a function of the determination of needs, from eating, dressing, bathing, toileting, medication management, personal hygiene, and daily check-ins. There is a dining area for residents (food can be brought to the individual's apartment if needed). Transportation is provided to go to the grocery store and/or special travel events. In addition to medicine monitoring & management, nurses and doctors may be available, according to a pre-arranged schedule. Other amenities may be available, such as a hair salon, activity room/gym and the ability to perform housekeeping & laundry. Some facilities allow small animals. The resident is generally allowed to furnish their own apartment. The facility may be able to help augment furnishing with additional specialized furniture.

There is the potential at some point, due to the incapacity of the individuals that the family may need to make the decision about the retirement facility in which to locate their parent/family member/friend who is no longer capable of handling this decision.

This decision may be the move from the family home to an assisted living facility, or perhaps moving from an assisted living facility to another one that has more care capabilities (such as memory care for those with Dementia-Alzheimer's). The family member making this decision should be prepared to visit a number of potential assisted living/memory care facilities before choosing one (the decision must be made quickly as often there are waiting lists for any facility). These are some suggestions in terms of what to look for/review:

- Seeing how the residents of the facility look – do they have clean clothes, good hygiene – well cared for hair, etc.?
- Were the residents wandering around aimlessly?
- Try to get references from other people who have a family member at the facility in consideration.
- Is the facility located in a safe neighborhood with good security measures in place?
- Will there be a requirement to share a room?
- Is the room available close to a nurse's station?
- Are there lots of activities for the residents?
- Are services available such as dentists, podiatrists, ophthalmologists', optometrists, who visit from time to time, or are nearby?
- Are vans available to take residents to doctor visits or other activities, including shopping?
- Are animals (small dogs or cats) allowed?
- Are dining areas clean and does the food look appetizing?
- Are there written procedures for all medicines to be dispensed, and careful monitoring of this process?
- Is there staff to cover 24 hour care availability?
- What is the availability of nurses?
- Is there the ability to augment care with contracted Care Givers?

As noted, the retirement housing transition decisions can be very stressful at each transitional point in the process, first moving out of the family home, then into a retirement facility, and then into a higher level assisted care facility. As with the health care concerns, the decisions can be difficult, changing as care needs change, and costly.

CHAPTER 7

ASSISTED LIVING

When the family home will no longer be an option, and a retirement/assisted living facility is the now a requirement, primarily due to health care issues and/or the need for (perhaps) round the clock care, the next stage of retirement begins; the need for assisted living. This will not be the case for everyone. Some may be able to stay in the family home. But the decisions noted below will, to some extent, be the same. For example, downsizing will likely be a benefit; as a previously large home, one with multiple bedrooms (for a family) will not be required any more. Downsizing will save money; money that may be necessary for living and health care expenses (care givers, prescriptions, etc.).

As the years progress, decisions will become more difficult and stressful for the retirees and the family & friends involved. Assuming that is it now time for leaving the family home of many years of residence, this is not a simple task. Moving only those things necessary to furnish a (generally) smaller residence or apartment in a retirement facility is a difficult task. Typically, items found in the home had been kept for many, many years. What should be kept now? What should be given away now? What will be needed for the future? Forcing the change and going through all the personal and household items now tends to occur when emotions and feelings are running to the extreme. There is a need for early resolution, when it has been decided to move into the retirement/assisted living facility. This forces the decisions to insure that all their items of necessity are sent to their new, smaller living area of the retirement facility. Storage facilities can store the extra items (for a while). The storage costs can start to add up and there are diminishing returns. Is the storage of old (useless) papers or nick-knacks really important – not likely? It is recommended that as soon as possible, go through the items in storage and make decisions about throwing items away, giving them away, selling or keeping them. Most items will never be used again. If they can be sold; great, then those monies can augment other retirement expenses now.

When moving into a retirement facility, most retirement/ assisted living facilities do not want the residents to cook – concern of a fire hazard for those that may forget something on the stove, so in many cases, there are no stoves. They may not want residents to have an injury due to the use of knives while cooking either. There may be a kitchenette, with cupboards, sink, and only one large appliance, a refrigerator. Thus, any previously used kitchen utensils, pots and pans can be part of the items given away, sold or thrown away. For those that liked to cook, or perhaps are used to preparing meals, this transition can be a difficult one. A discussion on this issue prior to moving into the retirement/ assisted living facility is recommended.

Regarding a retirement/assisted living facility, the costs of a facility that meets most individuals' idea of an appropriately nice, comfortable and well managed (clean, secure, safe, properly staffed – nurses available most hours) can be painstaking to find, and once found; are there apartments available at that facility? Often the situation is that there will be a need to be put on a waiting list, until someone living at the facility moves, passes away, or new areas are built. With the older generation percentage of the population growing every year, it is not likely that the number of facilities will be able to keep up with the demand in the future. This drives up the price of these facilities (supply and demand), which can be upwards of $6,000 per month ($72,000 per year). At this rate, for a 5 year stay, the costs can be more than the cost of a home that was sold to develop the monies necessary for such living accommodations. If there is a requirement for additional Care Givers due to advanced health care issues, it is easy to add another $3,000 per month, and now the costs are more than $100,000 per year. I doubt that most people understand this or have planned for such expenses. The problems related to retirement/assisted living facilities are:

- Finding a facility that has rooms and availability (especially one that meets one's criteria and expectations of something nice, perhaps close to the existing family home).
- The costs are high and continuing to grow, and with a high demand and not enough facilities available, often there are waiting lists.
- The costs of the individual apartment may not be the total cost. There may be additional costs relating to: medicines monitoring and distribution, routine checks of the apartment for those with significant health issues, special diets, having meals delivered to the room/apartment, etc.

Currently, no politicians are discussing the cost of the retirement care issue. Look for this to become a big issue within the next five-ten years. Will the federal government or states have monies to help the folks find a suitable retirement/assisted living facility? Not likely? Where will the people that need these, and perhaps cannot afford them go? The cost of care will be quite high, and along with all other necessities this can be a burden on the pocket book. It will likely be dangerous and unsafe for them to live at home alone. We'll talk about one issue specifically in Chapter 14: falling. This is a big concern especially for someone living alone.

One of the interesting things about residing in an assisted living situation is who enjoys it and who doesn't. Relative to couples, the individual that was always cared for by other, generally has no problems with this transition, as they have no problem continuing to be "waited on" in assisted living conditions. The one that previously may have prepared the meals, and perhaps was a Care Giver to the other spouse may miss what was normalcy of providing service and may not get used to residing in a place where service is now provided to them by others (staff). They may miss doing things for themselves. This may change later due to health issues, whereas they recognize that they are not able to perform care or cooking any longer, or they may forget that they once did perform such efforts, especially if they later develop Dementia-Alzheimer's, which will be discussed in great detail in Chapter 20.

Residing in an Assisted Living Facility has some critical and important aspects for consideration in order for a successful transition (from the family home). Downsizing to a smaller residence area, understanding a life style change, relying on others for care, and of course, the realization of the additional and necessary expenses of this assisted living.

CHAPTER 8

RETIREMENT COST EXTRAS

In an Assisted Living Retirement Facility, there are the potential of additional fees and extras, based upon health issues and concerns. The additional fees may include:

- Level of Assisted Living Services
- Fees for Pets
- Additional Personal Laundry
- Room Service of Meals – Trays brought to the Apartment
- Guest Meals
- Parking Places, if cars are still being used by residents.
- Additional Storage
- Safety Calling Devices – for falling & emergencies
- Additional Housekeeping
- Carpet Cleaning – a fall my turn into an unfortunate bloody event
- Multiple occupant fees
- Medicines management

Other fees may be assessed based upon health issues, concerns or physical capabilities*:

- Assistance with Bathing
- Multiple check-ins during the day
- Assistance with Toileting
- Specialty Meals
- Number of times medicines passed to resident – if more than one
- Vital signs checks
- Assistance with personal grooming
- Assistance with dressing
- Incontinence care
- Assistance with mobility/lifting/bedridden
- Assistance with use of a Walker
- Specialty nutrition/diet
- Assistance with feeding
- Additional consideration for a smoker
- Extra consideration for being a fall risk
- Assistance with Communication/Hearing Impairment
- Assistance with Skin Conditions
- Mental conditions: aggression, depression, wandering, sundowning
- Assistance with oxygen usage
- Medication Ordering

* Depending on an evaluation by the facility staff, the items above generally are given additive value/points, and based upon these needs; the additive valve/points could add hundreds of dollars to the monthly resident fees. Add in the amount for additional care givers, and it is easy to see that the annual costs rise to nearly $100,000 or more; just to sustain some quality of life. Again,

it is recommended that before anyone begin residency at any assisted care retirement facility, an evaluation of what fees may be assessed is understood. It is necessary and helpful to use in the development of an appropriate monthly/annual budget.

Note, for an individual suffering from Dementia-Alzheimer's the cost of residency alone can increase by over 50%, without adding on these other additional fees + care givers (likely). Now, the annual totals can be nearly $150,000.

CHAPTER 9

MANAGED CARE ISSUES & RECOMMENDATIONS

There are many aspects for managing care in retirement. Certainly the health related issues (including management of medicines, and use of Pharmacies) are critical. But there are other issues of concern related to managing care for all aspects of retirement living, from the Family taking control of finances to insuring the proper needs for specialized furniture.

Progressing through their retirement years, health issues certainly play a larger role in life. Doctor visits are certainly more frequent, as is the occasional need for hospital or emergency room care. Along with the various doctors, for various aspects of their health, comes the inevitable multitude of medicines. It becomes clear (later) or seemingly clear that perhaps the doctor's had decided to prescribe more and more medicines, as more and more health issues arise, such that eventually the individuals are taking a long list of prescription medicines. Taking more and more medicines puts them at more risk of dangerous side effects. Seemingly, for each health issue, it seems that the doctor's add another prescription to the list. Tracking this multitude of medicines must now be an important consideration (and/or monitored) by the care giver (at the retirement/assisted living facility – this is the part of the assisted living {costs}, where now the facility insures that the proper, and only proper medicines are handed out and taken by the residents) and hopefully properly monitored by the pharmacists whom are preparing the various medicines. Living at home means that someone needs to come in daily, perhaps multiple times in one day to monitor and hand out the medicines. This can be quite costly, and it is not easy. Whereas retirement facilities have staff dedicated to the monitoring and dispersing of medicines (additional costs are added to monthly fees); for those providing home care these would be additional costs also. In either case, mistakes (likely unintentionally) can be made, and this puts patients at risk, especially if they are taking a multitude of medicines at different times of the day or night, prescribed by different doctors. Again, this is a costly requirement of care and an important necessity of care at this age. If family is living close by, it is recommended that they continue to monitor the medicines as much as possible. For those without family to monitor, the risks are greater (understanding that everyone are trying to provide the best care), yet, mistakes can still be made. Everyone should have an updated list available of their prescriptions, and this updated list should be available to family, retirement facility staff, and Care Givers. One way of keeping track of this list of prescriptions is to have it noted on the "Notes" section of their smart phones. The bottom-line is to make sure that this prescription list is updated.

Another important decision (or need) is the requirement, for monitoring and/or dispensing of Prescription Drugs (and in some cases even "Over-the-Counter" Drugs). Some Over-the-Counter Drugs, like Cough Syrups, can be very dangerous, if taken more than the labels describe (this can easily occur if the individual forgot how much they consumed). In the Retirement/Assisted Living Facility, the dispensing of all drugs is done by nurses and/or the staff. This is done for the safety of the residents, to insure that the proper dosage is given each day. However, even in the structured, managed process of dispensing drugs, mistakes in dosages, amounts or even the drugs can occur. It is best (recommended) that the family review the medicines given from time to time to insure that the correct and latest prescriptions, as prescribed by the doctor, is what is dispensed. It is best that a copy of the medicines list be taken to all doctor's appointments, especially if there are multiple doctors providing care, thus any recent changes, or perhaps changes in health (mental or physical) can be discussed. Often the Retirement/Assisted Living Facility is responsible for the re-ordering of prescriptions, and they may not be aware of updates. Thus, updates of prescriptions must be shared with the Facilities directly, and the Facilities will require new prescription information; and an associated doctor's note for a change in frequency or dosage of ongoing medicines. Checking and rechecking by the family of the medicines taken is highly recommended. This is an important aspect for concern for the retirement facilities that everyone should be aware of and take steps to try to reduce the risks. The retirement facilities should have a plan that is shared with the family as to how mistakes are reduced or eliminated – double checking, re-reviewing daily, etc. If the Plan is not adequate or mistakes continue to be made, find another facility in which to live; as this is a critical, life or death situation.

Along with the medicines needed to deal with health issues, diet becomes a more important aspect of maintaining one's health. Certainly the amount and preparation of food becomes a concern. These are additional considerations relative to staying in the family home or moving into a retirement facility. Staying at home means that these meals must be successfully & safely prepared (perhaps by Care Givers brought in to perform this service), while moving into a retirement facility means that the staff will insure proper diet, the most healthy foods, and the proper amount on salt intake.

It is recommended that only one Pharmacy should be used for purchasing prescriptions to help reduce the chance that prescribed medicines from different doctors may have bad or serious interaction affects when mixed together. It is hopeful that the use of one single Pharmacy (that has programs that monitor these potential interaction affects) will reduce the chance of a serious or dangerous reaction to the wrong mixture of medicines.

There are so many issues in retirement & assisted living, that it is almost a requirement that someone of the Family be designated to oversee, manage and monitor the financial, health and living situation (typically this is the Successor Trustee {1st in line for decisions}, as spelled out in the Trust Documents. Between multiple doctors, multiple medicines/prescriptions (including the proper dosage), Care Givers, Retirement Facility Staff, Insurance, Medicare, routine bills, non-routine bills, management of costs and expenses (finances), and of course, health issues; it is nearly impossible for the Folks to do all of this and track everything themselves, especially if they are dealing with serious health issues. This is a full time job for those of the Family that help with all this and all the other minor issues that are related just to keep that essence of quality of life. If it is decided to continue to live in the Family Home, the issues are the same, perhaps more difficult when you add in the necessity of preparing (or having someone prepare the food) and take care of the Home itself, from gardening to laundry, cleanup to grocery shopping.

Whether living still in the Family Home (requiring augmented assistance by Care Givers), or in a Retirement/Assisted Living Facility (perhaps with an Internal Staff and perhaps also augmenting that with Care Givers), the Elderly are at risk of being taken advantage of. One unfortunate issue regards "Charities". Giving to Charities over the years has been a wonderful opportunity to help those in need. However, it also has resulted in putting them on Lists (that some Charities may share), where now multiple Charities will call asking for money, or send multiple mailings that clog mailboxes, where important papers and documents can be missed or misplaced. This can turn into a definite and unfortunate nuisance. Being on a "do not call" List can help reduce the multiple unnecessary phone calls. The multiple mailings is a difficult issue with little or no recourse for correction. This is another reason why the Family should take over the finances, such that these "Charities" are now managed properly and respectfully, but no longer with the Folk's contributions.

In addition to the "Charity" situation, there are other issues, including outright stealing of property and things. Since they have different individuals taking care of them, whether it is the Care Givers or Retirement/Assisted Living Staffs, they are at risk of having Jewelry, Money, and Antiques stolen. It is best if the family manages and plan for this and takes these items out of the family home or retirement/assisted living facility.

Certainly Cash, Checkbooks and Jewelry should not be left lying around, as these items can be taken by anybody without being seen. Now, there are times when the elderly may accuse Care Givers or (Retirement Home) Staff of taking things, and this too is a problem of concern. This too is another reason to remove any potential item (cash or jewelry) from being taken. If there is a need to keep a checkbook available, it should be hidden or perhaps in a safe. Family heirlooms or antiques should not be kept in a Retirement Facility or Family Home where Care Givers come and go, especially, small items that could be put in a pocket and taken. I am not saying that all Care Givers or (Retirement

Home) Staff are thieves or criminals, but it only takes one, and often the turn-over rate is often very high. Better to be safe than sorry. The Retirement Facility or Care Giver Company may have insurance to cover these thief's, but the issue is that it is nearly impossible to prove, unless cameras are installed in the Facility's Apartment or Family Home. This is an important reason why the removal by the Family and management of valuables is almost a necessity. Then, when the issue of a loss comes up (where a Care Giver is accused of a theft), and it will, the Family can share that they have taken custody of rings, watches, monies, etc. (thus, the Care Giver could not have taken the item).

Furniture is another significant item of consideration, which requires appropriate planning and management. If moving to a Retirement Facility or staying in the Family Home, likely a downsizing of the amount of furniture needs to occur or taken into serious consideration. Decisions on the proper furniture to have available is important. It may be difficult for them to get out of the cushy chair that they used to love. Now a decision needs to be made (and reviewed with their doctor) about a chair that has the option of raising the back to help with the process of exiting from the chair. There are pros and cons with this. If no longer having an opportunity to use those muscles, those muscles could atrophy, which is not a good thing. Certainly exercise at this age is important, even if it is just lifting oneself out of a chair.

Additionally, specialty beds may be required. If someone is a fall risk, and have the potential of trying to get up during the night, perhaps a hospital-like bed will be required that has rails. Other specialty beds may be required if there is difficulty getting in & out of bed (thus a need for lowing/raising the bed to accommodate this issue). A specialty bed may make it easier for the Care Givers to take care of their elderly patients, if they have incontinence (lacking control of bodily functions).

Managed care is an important aspect of retirement living. There are many factors to consider, such as insuring proper medicines and associated dosages are taken, management of finances & charitable giving, managing and securing personal items, and having the proper furniture.

CARE GIVERS

The elderly are dependent on Care Givers eventually at some stage of their lives. There can be different stages of "Care Giving". These are noted below:

- Stage One: The first stage will generally occur when one of the spouse's develops a significant health issue where the other spouse or a family member takes care of the individual with the health issue.
- Stage Two: Either the health issue becomes too difficult to handle, or the other spouse or family member is no longer capable to provide total care, and thus the care must be augmented by a professional "Care Givers". This may occur while the individual receiving the care is still in the family home or a retirement facility. If still in the family home, this Care Giver may be contracted to do light housework, cooking, and/or monitoring of medicines. If at a retirement facility, this Care Giver provides efforts related to more round-the-clock observations and support (monitoring of medicines may be part of the facility staff's obligations).
- Stage Three: With more significant physical and perhaps mental health issues, this Care Giver needs to have more

medical training, and perhaps more direct interaction with the individual that may be a "Fall" Risk. Perhaps the individual requires more monitoring and support for the physical (assistance with bathing, toileting) and mental issues. This stage also includes the inevitable time right before passing, where the Care Givers provide critical assistance with the more difficult aspects of care (such as getting out of bed, bathing, toileting, eating, monitoring oxygen equipment usage {for those that may have reduced lung capacity or difficulty breathing and thus a doctor has approved the equipment to assist with these issues}, etc., in order to make the Folks as comfortable as possible prior to passing.

So, who are the Care Givers? "Care giving in the U. S in 2009 (was) estimated at 43.5 million people, ages 18 and older are providing unpaid care for others age 50+. Three of four care givers work full-time while providing an average of 20 hours per week of assistance. Care giving is a demanding part-time job" (at least) and depending on the recipient's needs may become a full time job. "Nearly 10 million people over the age of 50 are caring for their aging parents (in 2012), according to a study conducted by the MetLife Mature Market Institute, in conjunction with the National Alliance for Caregiving and the New York Medical College. The number of care givers has more than tripled over the past 15 years. The increase reflects medical advances and the resulting increase in human longevity."[14]

The need for care giving assistance involves a number of reasons. As people get older, they often require help with basic daily tasks, such as getting dressed, eating, bathing, or getting in and out of beds or chairs. What's also important (if still living at the family home), recipient's need help keeping their households going, doing chores around the house, grocery shopping, paying the bills, and getting to doctor's appointments.

"Older adults take an average of five medicines daily, and 96 percent of all care givers ensure that their loved ones take the proper medicines, at the correct dosage, at the right time of day."

The cost of Elder Care is increasing, resulting in children providing financial assistance to their parents. Below is a table of the costs, according to a MetLife 2011 Market Survey of Long-Term Care Costs:

Type	Average	Annual
Nursing Home: Semi-private room	$214/day	$78,110
Nursing Home: Private Room	$239/day	$87,235
Assisted Living	$3,477/month	$41,724
Home Care: Home Health Aide	$21/hour	$21,840
Home Care: Homemaker	$19/hour	$19,760
Adult Day Services	$70/day	$18,200

Table 4-1[14]

Not only are the costs for elder care expensive, but the costs for the Family can have serious affects on their monies, not counting if they are augmenting care costs already. MetLife estimates, that "the lost wages due to dropping out of the labor force (to help an elderly family member) averages nearly $143,000"[9], which "reflects wages lost while not working (for about 5 years), as well as lower wages after returning to the workforce with rusty skills".[14] "When forgone pension and Social Security benefits are counted, the out-of-pocket losses roughly double."[14] "The total estimated aggregate lost wages, pension, and Social Security benefits of these care givers of parents/family are nearly $3 trillion."[9] "Some women's groups (women are typically the care givers by a wide margin) say that Congress should expand tax credits available to people with dependent relatives and create 'care giving credits' to limit the Social Security penalty for time spent out of the labor force to provide family care." An Indiana University reports says' informal care givers provide service that would otherwise cost the Medicare System (about) $375 billion a year'".[9]

Not only is the cost of providing care expensive, there are other costs too:" Again, according to MetLife, "adult children 50+ who work and provide care to a parent are more likely to have fair or poor health than those who do not provide care to their parents."[9]

According to the Rand Corporation, "the price tag for informal care giving of elderly people by friends and relatives in the United States comes to $522 billion a year". "Replacing that care with unskilled paid care at minimum wage would cost $221 billion, while replacing it with skilled nursing care would cost $642 billion annually." "(People) across America spend an estimated 30 billion hours every year providing care to elderly relatives and friends." "(There is) interest in workplace flexibility policies being considered by a number of states that provide paid time off from work for Care Givers, as well as programs such as Medicaid's Cash and Counseling Program that allows family care givers to be paid for their assistance."[14]

For the spouse, care giving at Stage 1 can take a toll (health wise) on the spouse that may not have the most serious health issue, resulting in more exaggerated health issues for the spouse whom had taken on the role of the care giver. Care givers need to be aware of this issue. Often the Care Giver can become exhausted and worn down, leading to a reduction in their own capabilities to fight off health issues, i.e. colds, which they would normally be able to avoid. But if their immune system is weakened, they themselves may require additional care. This puts their care giving capabilities at risk or at least on hold. Note, if the spouse is the care giver, they often have to put up with the difficulties related to the other spouse's health issues, and often deal with the mental anguish that a sick spouse may spew forth, even if not really meant to emotionally hurt the care giver. Many spousal care givers become the dutiful one that has to take the wrath of the other spouse. Some spouses may embrace this role of caretaker and it was a difficult one. The cost of Care giving (by a family member) can be substantial, as noted. Your days are filled with balancing work, the needs of your own family, and care giving responsibilities. There's no doubt this juggling act takes its toll. That's why it is so important to recognize when you're stressed, and to do something about it. Remember, if you don't take care of yourself, you can't take care of someone (who needs the help that) you love.

If family members become no longer available for care giving, then others must be brought in at Stage 2, with significant expense to take care of the individual that now requires the additional care above and beyond the normal aspects of life. Plans for the inevitably of having care givers should be considered during latter part of the retirement years.

Typically the Contracted Care Givers in Stage 2 may put in 4 - 8 hours of care, helping with chores, cleaning, making meals, or just being there for support. For the families of the folks that decide to stay at home, even with Care Givers coming in to help out, there is a toll on the family. Also, there needs to be a back-up plan, when a contracted caregiver is not able to come to the home for their regular shift. But mostly, the stress on the family involves dealing with the health issues, insuring that care givers take care of the necessities, and (unfortunately) watch out for the care givers that may take advantage of the situation. Not saying that all care givers (no matter working at a family home or in a retirement facility) steal from the elderly, but they certainly have the opportunity, and if their pay and hours are long, or the people are difficult to deal with, they may decide that they are "due" some extra pay in the form of removing some things that may not be theirs. This is unfortunate, but seems to happen in many instances, and no one can watch these folks every minute. Again, many are honest and are there to help the elderly. It is more likely that the elderly will lose things on their own or throw them away; not knowing the value, or remembering they threw it away, or that they tried to hide it. It is best to plan for this upfront as discussed earlier (and this is very important), and therefore remove all jewelry and valuables from the home or the retirement facility as soon as possible.

In Stage 3, the contracted Care Givers may be required for 8-12 hours of care, and this certainly adds substantial costs. This stage certainly requires a care giver with more training and experience, and thus the hourly rates reflect this. These Care Givers have much more responsibilities and are critical in monitoring the needs and potential emergencies.

Most Contracted Care Givers are wonderful, trustworthy and honest people that perform a difficult job, under the difficult circumstances of dealing with the elderly who are experiencing poor physical and mental health. However, it must be mentioned that even the "presumably" most kindly caregivers can have a dark side. This is why the family or friends must monitor the Contracted Care Givers from time to time. For some Care Givers can still be found that do not talk to the elderly in a respectful manner and may be even demeaning. Clearly, this is not acceptable and these Care Givers must be removed or fired as soon as possible. They may talk nicely while the family is visiting, but when they are alone with the elderly, they may treat them with disrespect. This occurs more often than one might think, as frustrations with the elder individuals may lead to this unfortunate situation. There are too many examples in the news of Care Givers abusing or hurting their elderly patients. The family must monitor the Contracted Care Givers from time to time to insure proper care is being performed at all times. The Contracted Care Givers must always be calm, understanding, forgiving (at times) and capable of handling difficult situations safely (monitoring health issues), quickly (perhaps to avoid a fall) and carefully (monitoring medicines); and with confidence and grace.

11

ELDERLY HEALTH CARE ISSUES

Health dominates nearly everything else during the retirement years and certainly in the latter part of those years. Some of the diseases & illnesses that can occur include: heart disease (note: even nose bleeds can be serious depending on the heart medications – blood thinners), cancer, diabetes, osteoporosis, and arthritis, all which certainly account for the major concerns. However, there are other health related problems at this age that can be troublesome, they include an UTI (urinary tract infection), pneumonia, and shingles which can be related more to age than anything else, and they can become very important in elder care, and the need to be addressed right away. Unfortunately, an UTI is something that may occur with poor hygiene. In general, UTI's are not contagious, and they start with the colonizing bacteria, like E coli. Individuals that have an UTI are generally isolated from other retirement facility residents, as a precaution, until they are deemed no longer infected. Certainly, a doctor's care and appropriate medicines are necessary if an UTI is contacted. An UTI can be a significant issue if not properly treated and improvement shown in a reasonable time. A doctor's knowledge of the situation and prescribing medicines to properly combat the UTI is important.

The onset of an UTI may be due to being rundown or due to loss of energy, which reduces the body's capability to fight off infections (such as an UTI). Females due to their physical makeup seem to be more susceptible to UTI's. Experiencing an UTI can result in the patient having a significant mood-swing or angry reaction to just about any issue, and it is the mood swing that is an indicator that they may have an UTI, and they (the family or Care Giver) should consider discussing the concern with a doctor.

Other health issues may now play a more significant role (not that these issues may not have earlier), such as sight & hearing problems. The sight & hearing issues can lead to stress in different ways. If one spouse has sight or hearing issues, and the other doesn't, the effect on any relationship can be stressed, as one may need to be careful with the noise levels (hearing) as not to be too soft or too loud. Hearing the phone or television and making adjustments to hear those devices can make for a stressful living situation, as the one with a hearing issue needs the higher volumes and the other may resent having to adjust to the higher volumes. Poor hearing has a great affect as one ages in a number of ways that will be discussed further in the next chapter on "Change". Worsening of sight and hearing in later years (in addition to reflexes) play a critical role in the decision about no longer driving or operating a motor vehicle.

More than ever, going to the doctor is an important part of this stage of life, especially in the management of these elderly health care issues. Many factors now play a more critical role with elder health care, such as needing to take multiple medicines without dangerous side effects, the need for monitoring of medicines (prescriptions and non-prescriptions) and the level of severity of the health issues, and having Care Givers and family monitoring the individual's medicines are taken correctly and be aware if bad side effects are experienced.

With the potential for increased or more serious health conditions, routine check-ups are important and necessary, not only with the doctor(s), but with the dentist. Another doctor to consider seeing, for the elderly, is the Podiatrist, since it becomes more difficult to be able to cut ones toenails, and it is important to look at the condition of the feet.

Health care issues during the later stages of life can play a significant role. Age-related health care concerns can dominate the retirement years. However, proper medical health care management and precautions can be taken to reduce some of the severity of the illnesses noted above. Certainly, appropriate diet, proper rest, good hydration and doctor-approved exercise may ward off more serious illnesses, or reduce their affects.

CHAPTER 12

DEALING WITH "CHANGE"

As the elderly reach their sixties and beyond, "Change" is one of the most difficult things to deal with for them and the family. Consideration of "Change" in later years becomes nearly unbearable and affects all aspects of their lives. With the technology changes' occurring now days, this results in both benefits and disadvantages for the older generation. Doing things the old way, a routine experienced for many years, may not even be available, or readily available any more. An example of this is banking, where on-line banking and bill payment is now the norm. There are fewer and fewer banks that continue with the old style of tellers and banking at the local establishment. Also, the need for immediate Cash has changed, where primarily; everything is accounted for using a credit card. Thus, taking out and using cash is no longer necessary. But when used to taking care of everything with Cash and Checks, this is not a welcome change. For some, credit cards were not even used. This was changed with the requirement for travel, where a credit card was required to procure a rental car. There are numerous examples of change now days from just a few years ago. With concentration on some of the changes that affect the older generation, Change is important and often causes stress and anxiety.

At times, anything related to "Change" is completely unacceptable. Financial decisions at this stage of life take on a critical role. With the unwillingness to change, discussions with family about financial issues can be difficult and stressful. Finances at this stage of life are really based upon the planning and actions prior to this stage of life. The finances are pretty much set now, and the issue becomes, will there be enough money to live on the rest of their lives, which could be another twenty or thirty years past the time they retired? What happens if the one's health deteriorates and requires even more care and more support is required to live a normal "quality of life" existence, more concerns than anyone really foresaw? Most people at this stage of life have been conservative with their money; they were careful with their finances and careful with their decisions. This conservatism can have advantages and disadvantages at this stage of life.

The advantages of conservative decisions are that they will not likely vary from the past ones. If financial planning was done in the past, it may still be effective now. However, if there are now unexpected costs or necessities due to health issues, or either spouse, that requires a modification or rethinking of finances, and that may now be a problem, made more difficult and stressful because it may result in a change; or a change from a conservative stance on the finances or living situation. If family, friends or children are involved in these decisions, the right place and time to discuss these issues must be determined, soon.

For most, making decisions now are nearly 100% based upon what had been done in the past. If it worked before, it must be right now, unless the old option is no longer available. The most difficult decisions are those that involve change or the need to make a change. Even minor insignificant decisions, for example, were change is now required, could result in maximum concern and worry about the outcome.

It is best if all decisions and dealings are very structured. Simple payment of bills, i.e. the phone bill (something still monitored and maintained by the retiree, unless family has taken over control of the bill payment) must be carefully explained and paid per strict instructions, as it was in the past. For example, the way the checks are written and placed within an envelope – have to be done a certain way and only that way. Dealing with "Change", means <u>not</u> having to deal with change. It is less stressful if change does not occur due to technology changes, as an example, a new TV must be one that is simple to operate (one with a remote that has multiple options is not acceptable, even to the point of having to return it to the store).

Fear of change can affect the decisions made. The elderly generally do not want to be a burden to anyone, or cause anyone to have to go out of their way to help them – they could take care of it themselves, they always had. But now, that situation was about to "change". Unfortunately, as people age, they are more prone to falling, as will be discussed in Chapter 14. There are devices that send alert signals for help when someone falls. However, many times, the elderly are concerned and don't want to bother anyone, and thus they are hesitant about calling for help, as they do not want to call the fire department or paramedics when they have a bad fall (no matter how close the fire department may be). This is an issue that should be discussed before a serious issue happens, especially if they are still living at home. This is a surprising situation. It appears that the thinking is that they are being a burden; this depending on others, even emergency personnel is a change from the norm and thus is difficult issue to deal with. It should be reminded that it is important that they call for the paramedics, when they fall, as not calling could result in minor injuries turning into serious health problems. These decisions to request timely help, at this age, are critical.

Any change from the routine is now an issue of considerable magnitude. An example occurs at retirement facilities, where they have dining rooms for the residents. The seating arrangements for each session of dining (if more than one) are such that there is nearly assigned seating, no changes, and anyone whom doesn't belong or tries to change seats is usually abruptly told not to do so – by the other retirement facility residents (not the retirement facility staff). The only exception to this rule is if children are visiting. They are able to have the seating changed, but still only slightly – maybe a chair or two is added to a table of residents.

Why is "change" such a huge issue? There are a number of factors that could affect this issue. Certainly, the worsening of individual's eyesight and hearing capacity contribute to the concern about change. If one can no longer insure that they can "see" everything down to a minute detail, it is easier not to deviate from something already established. Similarly, with hearing, if one can no longer fully "hear" what might be going on, it is better to not consider a deviation. It is reasonable to believe that this it is related to degradation of these two senses.

But there are other factors at this stage of life relative to "Change". If things worked previously ("if it ain't broke, don't fix it) is the feeling. Additionally, "change" will likely mean that something that seemed relatively secure now will no longer be safe and secure if changed (and this is a significant concern at this older stage of life). This is true, especially, if it is related to health or health care. For example, comments made by a doctor in the past are taken as "the gospel", and any deviation now is "obviously" wrong. This will play an even bigger role in later years, especially when new doctors are involved in the health care issues and decisions.

There is also a "Change" concern about institutional issues that may have a long standing in regards to the way things are done. This has an effect on the financial and health care decisions. This is the case, especially if things are spelled out in Trusts and Wills.

Updates to these Trust and Will documents become a difficult task (even if logical and the importance is obvious) because it wasn't done that way before. Note, often, laws relative to these documents or their ramifications are modified, requiring updates. Thus, a change may be required, but not acted upon without considerable decision and even hurt feelings by all involved. These are very stressful situations in trying to explain why modifications must be made as a result of new legislation or realization of potential legal problems to avoid, now or in the future.

Even small changes in the "routine" can result in significant stress. For example, at the grocery store, if you were to buy them groceries, the groceries have to be a certain brand and a certain type of packaging. At the restaurant, the food ordered does not vary much, and the way it was served also has to be the same. Buying a new shirt or jacket may not be successful, and one may be told to take them back, as the clothes that they have worn for years, are still "good".

The above are some of the easier decisions that are required to be made. There are decisions that are much more difficult, which often result in stress, and even anger, but require significant decisions and significant "Change". These decisions involve Finances, and especially how to manage them, and by whom. As discussed earlier, Trusts & Wills should already be in place by this point in life. That does not necessarily make it easier to discuss the passing of the finances, or payment of bills, on to the family for next and final stages of life. It is best to start with a transition of payment of some of the minor bills, i.e. the phone bill. Once it is seen that this transition is successful, they may be more willing to eventually have all the bills managed by the family (hopefully there are family members available to do this). It is recommended that the management of all finances be transitioned to the family as soon as possible. This reduces the risk of later stress and concern. With the possibility now days of identity theft, fraudulent schemes against the elderly, etc.; it is best that family handle the finances and reduce these risks. Hopefully, the family can carefully manage the budget for all the retirement expenses as necessary. This is not an easy task and can take considerable time and effort, especially as the health issues may worsen. Again, dealing with Health Insurance, Medicare, Social Security plus the Finances is nearly a full time job.

At these later stages of life, there are many changes that are going on and affect the lifestyle. If there is a move from the family home to a retirement/assisted living facility, this will be a significant change that some folks may enjoy, while others may regret. For a couple, where one likes the change, and the other wants to go back home (doesn't like the move), this can be the start or continuation of many argument on the subject. This puts the family in the middle of this argument, which is a difficult position. The family must continue to support the one that likes the move, emphasizing the benefits of the move, while emphasizing to the other the reasons why living at home is no longer feasible or enjoyable. This emphasis on the positive and the reality may not stop the argument (and the focus) on this change, but may reduce further stress.

Other significant and likely Changes include the removal of a vehicle (no longer needed) and thus the removal of the freedom to get around: travel, shopping, dining out, etc. This freedom to get around is a difficult situation to get used to, especially when for so many years this capability was available and taken for granted. Cutting off the ability to travel is an important change resulting in the (family) need to now plan for such things as getting or receiving groceries.

Since most retirement/assisted living facilities have dining rooms and eating areas, groceries for food items are no longer necessary. For those that may have cooked for themselves or the family for many years, this will mean a number of Changes. Going to the Dining Hall to eat meals is a significant Change. At first, they may feel that this dining hall experience is an uncomfortable one. Over time, and by getting a chance to meet and greet these other residents, this situation becomes more comfortable and thus a reasonable Change. Even the Food will involve change, as a consideration for all, means that the seasoning of the food may be more bland (i.e., without as much salt), this too is a Change that requires getting used to regarding their meals. Getting used to not cooking for themselves is a definite Change. Not even having the capability to cook (most resident apartments in the retirement/assisted living facilities do not have stoves, ovens or even microwaves) as a safety precaution, yet another change.

In later life, Physical and Mental Change are now major considerations. The ability to take care of one-self is significant. Is there a need for assistance to shower and bathe them-selves? Is assistance needed to go to the bathroom, or now must they wear adult diapers? Do they need assistance to get out of bed, or get up from a chair? The mental Change will be discussed later relative to Dementia-Alzheimer's (reference Chapter 20). But the physical and mental changes result in aguish and stress. This aguish and stress can result in emotional and difficult times for family, friends or care givers, when aggravated comments, even cursing occurs. I believe that they do not really mean to express their unhappiness this way, often bluntly to others; it is just a function of these physical and mental changes that they are experiencing and the way they are coping with the situation.

"Change" is one of the most difficult issues of aging. Dealing with change, not understanding the need to change, and having to live with physical and mental (health) changes is significant and stressful. Anticipating that change is inevitable will hopefully help the family and Care Givers to minimize (as much as possible the stresses related to change). This can be done by pre-planning of upcoming changes, having discussions on the importance and logical reasons for change, and resolving issues or changes quickly, quietly, safely and effectively.

CHAPTER 13

MOOD SWINGS & PERSONALITY CHANGES

As people reach retirement age and especially during the later years of retirement, their health issues will take on a major emphasis in their existence and everyday living. But there are other things that occur that are important to understand. A potentially significant change at this stage of life is mood swings and/or a shift in personality.

This shift in mood may occur and be noticeable as a tendency to get upset, get loud and even yell. This situation can occur even for individuals that (in the past) where not of this temperament. Sometimes when making a point that they want to stress, rather than addressing the issue in a normal voice, all the sudden they may loudly and angrily express their concern. This may come up at any time for any issue, and generally does so more often. Perhaps, they are getting loud due to hearing loss, however, when they have this tendency to get loud, their hearing at the time may not be an issue (they can hear just fine). Perhaps with the hearing loss, they believe that getting loud is what they now believe is required to be understood. Sometimes this loudness and anger may be part of a mood swing; where things are just fine, and then for some unknown reason, there is a change in the way they are feeling and talking, and they may raise their voice to a much louder level, even shouting. It is almost like the youngster trying to get attention.

Mood swings may result in a very angry discussion suddenly. Other times the mood swings reflect a very defiant attitude. If reviewing family issues, they may take a very defiant stance on the issue, and mention how they know better. Often these angry and defiant expressions are related to any kind of suggested "Change". As discussed in Chapter 12, "Change" is a huge issue and any recommendations for "Change" should be carefully presented by Care Givers and/or family prior to broaching the subject. The Care Givers and family should be ready for an angry response for any mention of a situation involving "Change". In the past, when they were younger, they likely did not act this way. It is believed that they do not realize, at this stage in their lives, the way they are acting, thus it is important for the Care Givers and family to understand this and not get upset with them. This is extremely important. Care Givers and family must understand that there will be times when they will get angry, unpleasant, upset and downright defiant. It is best that Care Givers and family let them vent, and perhaps remove themselves temporarily from the situation and come back in a few minutes when they have calmed down. When returning, it is best to change the topic of conversation, or whatever may have been occurring, that may have resulted in the unpleasantness. There have been reports in the news recently where care givers got physical with the elderly that were in their care. Perhaps, it was during one of these incidents of angry outbursts.

There could be some very good reasons for these mood swings: (1) reluctance to "Change" or deal with "Change" issues, (2) a feeling that they are being told what to do, which means that they are no longer controlling what they do, thus the defiance,

(3) general health issues – they just do not feel well, (4) specific health issues – sight or hearing loss, or (5) the medicines that they are taking could cause them anxiety (as a side effect). One mood swing to be careful of, where the folks may have a significant and unknown change in mood, could be related to an "UTI", an Urinary Tract Infection, as discussed in Chapter 11. As noted, it is a significant issue for the older generation and can only be corrected with the proper medicines over time.

In addition to the Mood Swings (which can occur because of a UTI or due to Dementia-Alzheimer's), there can be a Personality Change at these later stages of the retirement years. It almost is as if they are given truth serum, as they tend to say things about others that they wouldn't have likely said in years past. They seem to have no problem in expressing their opinion on an issue whether it is politically correct to do so or not. This is why when the elderly are out in public, you may hear family members try to "shh" them. It may be a function of the reduced capacity to hear clearly, but it seems that they also want to do more shouting or yelling, as noted, especially when it comes to something that they do not like, or want to raise the level of attention. Often Care Givers or Retirement Facility Staff must counter these loud outbursts (outbursts that never would have happened in the past). Unfortunately, it may make the Care Givers or Staff, no option but to get loud also. This is not elder abuse; it is sort of like telling a teenager to be quiet. Of course if this continues, by the Care Givers or the Staff, decisions and discussions must occur to see how this can be stopped, before it does become abuse. I am not saying that the Care Givers or Staff are abusive, they just need some way to calm the situation, and this is not easy. Again, it is usually the elderly that are the ones that are raising their voices in a shouting manner. They must be told that this is not acceptable. All of this can be a function of these mood swings.

14

FALLING

There is a lot of talk about the issues of the elderly "falling" especially when they reach their 60's. It is indeed a significant issue for them, even when precautions are made. The bottom line is that the elderly will fall at some point. The hope is that the injuries that result will be insignificant and not life threatening. Prior to reaching their 60's, and even before, the elderly do not seem to believe that falls may occur and how to deal with them. The first significant falls will change this feeling, but the way it is dealt with may be surprising. When the first of the significant falls occurs, there is a distinct possibility that no one will be called, even if the fall is a bad one, with serious injuries and bleeding. The interesting thing is that the elderly <u>may not</u> want to call for help at "911". Sometimes it takes insistence from the family to get them to call the paramedics, when this happens at the family home. For the spouse/partner, when they do call family (not paramedics), they may comment that the other spouse/partner had fallen, may even be bleeding, and yet family is told that the other spouse was probably ok, and there was no need to bother anyone. Of course this is the wrong course of action. It may not matter that local paramedics are only a couple of blocks away, and would be happy to help them. Family needs to state that if they do not call "911", that the family will. It is not understood why they do not want to call the emergency phone line, and it is an issue that many of the elderly seem to have. It seems that this is another "Change" issue, another change in lifestyle that is not comfortable, as they need to depend on others, not previously used, especially paramedics. It is recommended that family have a conversation about falling before it occurs, such that this issue about calling "911" is less likely to be a concern. Every time they fall at this age, they should consider calling, as internal injuries could occur and may not be noticeable right away. After a significant fall, calling "911" is the proper thing to do and helps to reduce the risk of perhaps minor injuries turning into serious injuries. Even minor injuries may require a short hospital stay. This is especially important for those that have heart conditions and may be taking heart medicines, which include blood thinners. In this case, each fall is significant and potentially a life-threatening event, requiring the need of proper follow-up at the local hospital/emergency room to be checked out (to insure that there is no internal bleeding or broken bones).

There is not much that can be done to reduce the chance of falling, as often it involves a situation that was routine, but with a wrong twist or turn, and down they go. Of course, ridding the home of "throw" rugs or small furniture certainly reduces the risks. These are the objects in the home that may contribute to falling. However, keeping physically fit is also important in reducing the possibility of a fall. Thus, exercise and stretching are very important and gives them the opportunity, should a slip occur, where perhaps they can catch themselves and thus eliminate the unfortunate fall. It is strongly recommended, with their doctor's approval, that proper exercise and stretching is a routine followed for the rest of their lives. This can be done in the family home (perhaps supervised with caregivers) or at the retirement/assisted living facility (which is likely to be supervised). Increased mobility results in fewer falls.

One of the most dangerous aspects of life in retirement is the potential for falling. It is almost guaranteed that they will fall. On the commercial on television, the statistics are quoted that after age 65; there is a greater than 60% chance that they will experience a serious fall. The potential for falling can occur at any time, walking indoors or outdoors, and the highest potential is in the bathroom, primarily getting in and out of a shower or tub. However, the chance of a fall is nearly constant, and the outcome of such a fall can be catastrophic, from broken bones to serious cuts and bruises, and if on heart medication that promotes circulation, even a minor cut can lead to serious loss of blood. All falls must be taken serious and investigated for potential internal issues, even if the signs of an internal problem are not obvious. With the fragile nature of bones at this age (due osteoporosis, or arthritic conditions), any fall could result in a broken bone, and the individual may not know that they have a broken bone.

Falling at a Retirement Facility should result in the contacting of the Staff, to determine if the individual needs medical attention or even a trip to the Emergency Room. If still living in the Family Home, a plan should be developed for dealing with "Falls". The wearing of the bracelets for calling help is certainly something that should be done. If not willing to wear the bracelet, any fall should be considered serious and help requested, including a call to 911.

There are devices that can be worn for those people that are serious fall threats. One such device is a belt, like the ones worn by karate students, that is wrapped around the individual. Then, any time that they start to walk around or get out of a chair, a Care Giver or family member can hold on. Of course this requires nearly 24 hour care and trained Care Givers, which is a much higher level of care.

Even with all these precautions, it just takes one second to have the unfortunate fall happen. And unfortunately when, not if, the fall occurs, it is time for strong measures of care consideration, immediately assessment of any injuries, and the need for further medical or emergency care, including the call to 911. This is the scenario every time, now.

15

HOSPITALIZATION & NURSING HOMES

The potential for more hospitalization is greater with age. Being ready for this situation is important. Being ready means: having a list of medicines taken readily available for review by the admitting hospital staff; having any diet restrictions known and able to also be passed on to the hospital staff; having the Advanced Health Care Directive available (to go with the elderly patients), as they leave for the hospital, or can be given to any ambulance. If it is typical that the same Hospital will be used in the majority of health care hospitalization, it may be possible to give a copy of the Advanced Health Care Directive directly to the Hospital prior to any visit, so that they can have it on file. Another new option here is to have an Advanced Health Care Directive Card in a Purse or Wallet, thus readily available for any Hospital that may be used for this care.

The decision process for considering going to the Hospital can be a difficult one. With Care Givers, if still living at home, or Care Givers augmenting a Retirement Facility Staff, the family needs to insure that they (the Family) be contacted in the review of the potential need for Hospitalization. If not able to be contacted, all Care Givers should have specific instructions in the determination of when the folks are in a situation where hospitalization (based upon health history) is the best course of action, and thus an ambulance is called to transport. Without the ability to contact the family, the Care Givers should be able to make the conservative decision, which is likely to have them checked out at the Hospital or Emergency Room. The Care Givers and the Family are the best ones for making the proper decisions at this stage of life, as the individuals may not have all their mental capabilities to know what is going on and what is the best course of action.

Though the Hospital Care is critical, important and life-sustaining, it does have its risks too. Multiple trips to the Hospital could result in the increased potential of contacting another disease through even unknown exposure, thus the more trips to the Hospital, the higher the risk of a significant mistake or fatal error. There are chances that mistakes can be made in the distribution of medicines, etc., at Hospitals due to the fact that the hospital may not have all the information on their new patient, perhaps they do not have all the information on their medical history (thus the critical importance of the updated list of medicines currently taken to thus reduce the possibilities of problems). This is not to say that the Hospitals will not provide superior care, they usually do; however, when they have all the patient history and information, information on medicines, etc., they certainly will be able to provide the best and proper care. The family can assist in getting the information to the hospital as soon as possible.

Often longer hospitalization care means the transport to a Nursing Home, away from the Hospital. These locations can have less experienced and smaller staffs. The family should consider this and thus monitoring should be more frequent to insure proper care. All of the precautions noted above are the same for a Nursing Home.

As previously discussed, but it is important to reiterate, the chances of needing some sort of Hospitalization at various times are very high, and in deciding a location of a Retirement Facility, the closeness of a Hospital should be taken into account. It is likely that a visit to a Hospital will be somewhat routine, usually to an Emergency Room or equivalent. Again, this is something that could be pre-planned for the inevitability of an occurrence, such that all of their medical history is readily available.

CHAPTER 16

MEDICAL INSURANCE & PRESCRIPTIONS

In all of the retirement years, medical issues and medicines play a significant role in everyday life. Dealing with the medical issues and the associated prescriptions is a critical aspect of successful health management, along with the associated costs. The Medical Insurance Plan Options should be carefully studied by the Family to determine the best course of action. Medicare plays an important role, but not the only role for elder health care.

There are Insurance Plans that are specifically dedicated to the people that are also on Medicare. These are: PDP (Prescription Drug Plan), HMO (Health Maintenance Organization) and PPO (Preferred Provider Organization) Plans.

A Medicare prescription drug plan (PDP) may help lower your prescription drug expenses and protect against higher costs in the future. However, you can't get prescription drug coverage through Original Medicare. Stand-alone prescription drug plans are only offered by private companies—like Humana—that have a contract with Medicare to provide them. Each plan provides coverage for a specific Drug List, called a formulary. Choose your plan carefully to make sure that it covers the medicine they regularly take, according to the Humana Insurance Company.

A health maintenance organization (HMO) is an organization that provides or arranges managed care for health insurance, self-funded health care benefit plans, individuals, and other entities in the United States and acts as a liaison with health care providers (hospitals, doctors, etc.) on a prepaid basis, as defined by Google.

For health insurance in the United States, a preferred provider organization (or PPO, sometimes referred to as a participating provider organization or preferred provider option) is a managed care organization of medical doctors, hospitals, and other health care providers who have agreed with an insurer or a third-party, again, as defined by Google.

The level of coverage is something to consider based upon their medical needs and health history. It is recommended that an insurance broker (independent or company representative) be consulted in order to get the best coverage for the circumstances. There are many options based upon cost and coverage for consideration. Additionally, be cognizant of deadlines for making the decisions for the coverage for the upcoming year. Again, hopefully there is a family champion (perhaps the Successor/1st trustee) taking the lead for the option decisions available with all the aspects related to Insurance. Along with the items listed above, people can have Supplemental Insurance Plans.

Here is one of the major issues that most experience, which plan pays first when you have other insurance coverage? When you have other insurance plans (like employer group health coverage) in addition to Medicare, there are rules set by Medicare that determine which insurance pays first. The insurance that pays first is called the "primary payer" and pays up to the limits of the coverage. The one that pays second, called the "secondary payer" only pays if there are costs left uncovered by the primary coverage. The secondary payer may still not pay all of the uncovered costs.

These rules apply for the employer or union group health plan coverage:

- If you have retiree coverage, Medicare pays first.
- If your group health plan coverage is based on your or a family member's current employment, who pays first depends on your age, the number of people employed by your employer, and whether Medicare based on age, disability or End-stage Renal (Kidney) Disease (ESRD):
    - If you're under 65 and disabled and you or your family member is still working, your group health plan pays first if the employer has 100 or more employees or at least one employer in a multiple employer plan that has more than 100 employees.
    - If you're over 65 and you or your spouse is still working, your group health plan pays first if the employer has 20 or more employees or at least one employer in a multiple employer plan that has more than 20 employees.

- If you have Medicare because of ESRD, your group health plan will pay first for the first 30 months after you become eligible for Medicare.

These types of coverage usually pay first for services related to each type:

- No-fault insurance (including automobile insurance)
- Liability (including automobile insurance)
- Black lung benefits
- Worker's compensation

Always, if you have "other" insurance, tell your doctor, hospital or pharmacy. If there are questions about who pays first, again, talk with the (insurance broker -independent representative or company representative). [4]

Keeping track of all this is not an easy task and errors can be made by the Insurance Companies or Medicare (not on purpose, but just due to the complications of it all).

Seriously, expect to spend hours and hours dealing with Insurance and Medicare Issues, while the Folks are living and even when they have passed. Hopefully, the Family is able to support this effort. Without a "Champion" (someone leading the charge), I do not know how people can handle all these issues by themselves.

What is covered by Insurance (including supplemental that may not be covered by Medicare), and what is covered by Medicare is not a simple question? What Medicines are covered? What Medicines/Prescriptions are covered as "Generics" only? What Medical Procedures are covered? What tests are covered – i.e. MRI's? What Surgeries are covered? How long does the billing take? Why are billing mistakes made? This all can be a nightmare and as noted above, take hours and hours to resolve, on the phone with the Insurance Carriers and Medicare, with follow-up letters, and then more phone calls and more letters. And, if not difficult enough, there are changes that occur in the coverage every year, so the family (champion) must stay aware of the new coverage also.

CHAPTER 17

MEDICARE

At this stage of retirement life, a critical aspect of life and health is now being at the age where Medicare becomes an important concern and dilemma. Not only are the prescriptions and the approval of such prescriptions important and the monitoring of these prescriptions critical; also there are the issuance of payments and the proper accounting for those payments. Doctor and hospital care, as covered by Medicare, can be a difficult and time consuming in terms of figuring and insuring proper coverage. With health care plans still available for some people (these plans may continue into retirement), both the Insurance Plans and Medicare must be reviewed and considered in order to determine the availability and consideration of care, and the payment of that care. Additionally, the relationship between Social Security Benefits and Medicare must be reviewed annually to insure appropriate alignment of payments and benefits. Social Security is very much a case by case scenario based upon the individual's past payments into the system, disability issues (if appropriate), age, etc.

Relative to Medicare, "2015 marked the 50th anniversary of Lyndon B. Johnson signing into law the Medicare Program/ Medicare that has been protecting the health and well-being of American families and saving live for five decades. Over the years, Medicare has grown, and as of 2015, provides quality health coverage for more than 50 million Americans", according to the 2016 <u>Medicare & You Guide,</u> as reported by the "Centers for Medicare & Medicaid Services" from the U. S Department of Health and Human Services' Handbook[3].

According to the Guide, you need to "understand your benefits and bills"[3] - not an easy task. One must understand and "learn how Medicare works".[3] "Medicare is health insurance for people 65 or older, people under 65 with certain disabilities, and people of any age with End-Stage Renal Disease (ESRD) (permanent kidney failure requiring dialysis or a kidney transplant)".[3]

It is important to understand the different parts of Medicare in order to understand what is covered, how payment of bills are made, and thus the effect on one's individual situation, or in this case, for a family Care Giver/Champion what is covered. There are four "parts of Medicare:

- Medicare Part A, which is a Hospital Insurance that (helps) cover:
    ○ Impatient care in Hospitals
    ○ Skilled nursing facility care
    ○ Hospice care
    ○ Home health care
    ○ Impatient care in a religious nonmedical health care institution

- Medicare Part B, which is a Medical Insurance, that (helps) cover:
    ○ Services from doctors and other health care providers
    ○ Outpatient care
    ○ Home health care

- o Durable medical equipment
- o Some preventive services

- Medicare Part C, which is Medicare Advantage, which:
  - o Includes all benefits and services covered under Part A and Part B
  - o Usually includes Medicare prescription drug coverage (Part D) as part of the plan
  - o Run by Medicare-approved private insurance companies
  - o May include extra benefits and services for an extra cost

- Medicare Part D, which is Medicare prescription drug coverage:
  - o Helps cover the cost of prescription drugs
  - o Run by Medicare-approved private insurance companies
  - o May help lower your prescription drug costs and help protect against higher costs in the future"[3]

All the above information is straight out of the 2016 Guide on Medicare. It behooves one, and especially the family Care Giver/Champion to understand the nuisances above. But, note the language used above: "helps cover", not "covers"; "some services/drugs" – it is important to determine whether the service or drug is covered before going further with the service, unless it is covered by a health insurance plan; "usually includes" – again look into whether the drug or a generic option is covered by Medicare or the health insurance. Also, investigate which one will actually pay for Medicare (Part A & Part B), as things change yearly including the Medicare premium and deductible amounts (meaning that the individual will need to be able to make up the difference, or have a health plan or insurance that covers what Medicare doesn't. Understand that "Medicare health and drug plans can make changes each year – things like the cost, coverage, and which providers and pharmacies are in their network. Also, be aware that, "Medicaid is a joint federal and state program that helps pay for certain health service for people with limited income and resources."[3]

"As always, if you have specific questions about Medicare, visit Medicare.gov to find the answers you need. You can also call 1-800-MEDICARE (1-800-633-4227)."[3] Do not be surprised if you have to wait on the phone for a while to get through, thus the Internet may be faster for general questions. Do not be surprised by billing snafus that occur and are discovered month's after the fact.

Some of the Medicare Part B Preventive Services include:

- Yearly "Wellness" visit
- Abdominal aortic aneurysm screening
- Alcohol misuse screening and counseling
- Bone mass measurement (bone density)
- Breast cancer screening(mammogram)
- Cardiovascular disease (behavioral therapy)
- Cardiovascular disease screenings
- Cervical and vaginal cancer screening
- Colorectal cancer screenings
    - Multi-target stool DNA test
    - Screening fecal occult blood test
    - Screening flexible sigmoidoscopy
    - Screening colonoscopy
    - Screening barium enema

- Depression screening
- Diabetes screening

- Diabetes self-management training
- Flu shots
- Glaucoma tests
- Hepatitis B shots
- Hepatitis C screening test
- HIV screening
- Lung cancer screening
- Medical nutrition therapy services
- Obesity screening and counseling
- Pneumococcal shot
- Prostate cancer screenings
- Sexually transmitted infections screening and counseling
- Smoking and tobacco use cessation counseling

Again, expect to spend hours dealing with the nuisances of Health Insurance Plans and Medicare. These are important benefits that unfortunately are difficult in their execution.

18

PERCENT OF POPULATION THAT IS ELDERLY

As previously noted, Health Care is probably the most talked about issue of our time. But the discussion has not effectively included the issue of elder care (excluding Medicare) and the increasing costs of this care. With the "Baby Boomers" reaching retirement age and beyond, this issue will be a critical one very soon, and <u>no one</u> is talking about it. But they will soon.

With some of the costs noted in the previous Chapters, who will pay for the millions of dollars that are needed for this care? With an economy that has been though difficult times recently, who will pay for those that have not had the ability to save for this level of care, yet need it? What will be done with those Folks? I do not believe that the Government can afford the costs for millions of elderly citizens, let alone where do they go for the assisted living issues they may need?

Now, for the statistics, according to the U. S. Census Bureau[5]: "Between 2012 and 2050, the United States will experience considerable growth in its older population. In 2050, the population aged 65 and over is projected to be 83.7 million, almost double its estimated population of 43.1 million in 2012. The baby boomers are largely responsible for this increase in the older population, as they began turning 65 in 2011. By 2050, the surviving baby boomers will be over the age of 85.

The projected growth of the older population in the United States will present challenges to policy makers and programs, such as Social Security and Medicare. It will also affect families, businesses, and health care providers and insurers.

By 2030, more than 20 percent of U. S. residents are projected to be aged 65 and over, compared with 13 percent in 2010 and 9.8 percent in 1970. (The reasons for the increase in the percentage are that) survivorship rates have shown improvement for many decades. In the United States, life expectancy at age 65 was 15.2 years in 1972 and rose to 19.1 years in 2010 – a gain of 3.9 years. (There are some) important trends (for this improvement and a significant one) is the reduction in smoking. A lifetime of smoking greatly reduces old-age survival. In 1970, 45 percent of the population aged 25 to 44 smoked (this is the population aged 67 to 86 in 2012, according to the American Lung Association in 2011. In 2011, only 22.1 percent of those aged 25 to 44 smoked (this will be the population aged 64 to 83 in 2050). This is good news and bad news. With the increase in the percent of the aged population increasing, there will be a great stress on the capacity of the elder care institutions (hospitals, assisted living facilities, retirement homes, care givers, etc.) that are setup to take care of this age group. This means that there will be an increased dependency of the older population on the next generation and the associated elder care institutions. Will we be ready for this scenario?

CHAPTER 19

PERCENT OF HEALTH CARE ISSUES FOR THE ELDERLY

Take as an example, being an octogenarian (living in their eighties), Health is of prime concern and as best as possible, maintaining some quality of life, is the goal. This can be difficult because of the natural aging process, which leads to a more sedimentary lifestyle. They may not be interested in exercise, but it is extremely important, as noted previously.

Significant healthcare issues at this stage of life include: heart disease, diabetes, pneumonia (the concern is to avoid it at all costs), respiratory disease, cancer(s), incontinence, shingles (again, something to avoid, and can be with shots), urinary tract infections (UTI) and Dementia – Alzheimer's. Relative to the most serious of the Health issues in 2013, the Leading Causes of Death of persons age 65 and over where: Heart Disease, Cancer and Chronic Lower Respiratory Disease.

According to the CDC (Centers for Disease Control and Prevention[6], relative to "Older Person' Health", as report from Health, United States 2014, the number of residents age 65 and over was 44.7 million in 2013. In 2013, the Life expectancy for men at 65 years was another 17.9 years, and for women, another 20.5 years. The percentage of non-institutionalized persons at age

65 and over in fair or poor health was 23.1% in 2013 (nearly 10 million). Based upon a <u>National Health Interview Survey</u> in 2013, the percentage of non-institutionalized persons at age 65 and over who need help with personal care from other persons was 7.2% (nearly 3 million).

Now there are some reasons for the poor health. Again from <u>Health, United States 2014</u>, the percentage of non-institutionalized persons at age 65 and over who currently smoke cigarettes was 8.8% (nearly 4 million). Relative to Obesity (2209-2012), the percentage of non-institutionalized persons at age 65 and over who are obese:

- Men age 65-74: 36.4%
- Men age 75 and over: 27.4%
- Women age 65-74: 44.2%
- Women age 75 and over: 29.8%

Relative to Diabetes, the percentage of non-institutionalized persons at age 65 and over with Diabetes (physician diagnosed and undiagnosed, 2009 - 2012) was 26.8%.

Relative to Hypertension, the percentage of non-institutionalized persons at age 65 and over with hypertension (measured high blood pressure and/or taking anti-hypertensive medication, 2009-2012) are:

- Men age 65-74: 61.7%
- Men age 75 and over: 75.1%
- Women age 65-74: 66.7%
- Women age 75 and over: 79.3%

Based upon the above information, the care services are already stretched to the limit, as the data shows:

- For Ambulatory care visits (to physician offices, hospital outpatient and emergency departments in 2010) by persons age 65 and over: 298.4 million.
- For Hospital Inpatient Care: the number of discharges from non-federal short-stay hospitals by persons age 65 and over: 13.6 million in 2010. And the length of stay in nonfederal short-stay hospitals by persons age 65 and over: 5.5 days.

Relative to Long-Term Care Services, the percentage of services' users who are 65 and over breakdown as follows:

- Percentage of adult day services center participants: 63.5% in 2012.
- Percentage of home health agency patients: 82.4% in 2011.
- Percentage of hospice patients: 94.5% in 2011.
- Percentage of nursing home residents: 85.1% in 2011.
- Percentage of residential care community residents: 93.3% in 2012.

Thus, the situation, based upon the statistics, individuals will likely require additional care and extended services related to that care whether it is anywhere from day services to residential care to augmented full-time care givers, and eventually hospice. Those that aren't planning for these scenarios may want to think about the planning to cover the potential for additional costs associated with these services.

20

DEMENTIA – ALZHEIMER'S

Dementia - Alzheimer's Defined, and what happens when a Loved One goes through the Stages of the Disease (the designated "stages" noted below are the opinion of the author)

I will refer to Dementia – Alzheimer's together in all due respect to those that have this disease. According to the <u>Alzheimer's Association</u>[7], Alzheimer's is defined as "a disease that attacks the brain. It is the most common form of dementia. Alzheimer's is a type of dementia that causes problems with memory, thinking and behavior. Alzheimer's disease accounts for 60 to 80 percent of dementia cases. Alzheimer's is a progressive disease, where dementia gradually worsens over a number of years. Alzheimer's is the sixth leading cause of death in the United States. Those with Alzheimer's live an average of eight years after their symptoms become noticeable to others, but survival can range from four to 20 years, depending on age and other health conditions. (Whereas) "Dementia is a general term for a decline in mental ability severe enough to interfere with daily life". (The) "Stages show how the disease unfolds, but progression will vary greatly from person to person".

"Alzheimer's has no current cure, but treatments for symptoms are available and research continues, and some treatments can temporarily slow the worsening of (the) dementia symptoms and improve the quality of life for those with Alzheimer's and their caregivers. The most common early symptom of Alzheimer's is difficulty remembering newly learned information, because Alzheimer's changes typically begin in the part of the brain that affects learning. As Alzheimer's advances through the brain it leads to increasingly severe symptoms, including disorientation (one item discussed later is the 'sundowner' effect), mood and behavior changes, deepening confusion about events, time and place, unfounded suspicions about family, friends and professional caregivers ('they stole my ring'), more serious memory loss and behavior changes; and difficulty speaking (clearly), swallowing and walking".

"Scientists believe Alzheimer's disease prevents parts (of the brain's cells from) processing, storing information and being able to communicate effectively. Two abnormal structures called plaques and tangles are (the) prime suspects in damaging and killing nerve cells (that result in the) memory failure and other symptoms of Alzheimer's. Ninety percent of what we know about Alzheimer's has been discovered in the last 15 years". The research and conclusions about the cause and treatment of Alzheimer's is controversial; and in some cases, very controversial, i.e., Alzheimer's is caused by the use of 'Aluminum'.

(Relative to Dementia, it) "Is often incorrectly referred to as 'senility' or 'senile dementia' which reflects the formerly widespread but incorrect belief that serious mental decline is a normal part of aging". Twenty plus years ago, older individuals were just considered 'senile', which we now know is dementia. There is not a particular age or reason when one can expect the onset of Dementia-Alzheimer's.

When a Loved One goes through the Stages of the Disease

Dementia – Alzheimer's is a disease that is cruel and the level of the disease increases rapidly over time. It does not increase exponentially, but it does have a steady worsening affect on the individual. There may be some medicines that slow the increased rate of the illness, but to-date, as noted, there does not appear to be a medicine that negates or reverses the effect.

Dementia – Alzheimer's starts with the simple loss of memory of a few general everyday items or facts, for example, forgetting where one placed their car keys or their wallet, or forgetting someone's name (someone that they normally would have no trouble remembering). This I will refer to as Stage 1. Of course, this does not mean that if one forgets where they put their keys, they are at the first stage of Dementia – Alzheimer's disease. This is only means that, once the disease has been diagnosed (more likely at Stage 2 or 3), that this is likely when it started.

Dementia – Alzheimer's next stage consists of more memory loss regarding more and more in dealing with general everyday items and perhaps how they work, for example, the working of a stove, car or the television. This stage can result in some dangerous situations, and thus the need for Care Givers must be considered. Certainly, the removal of the individual from cooking or driving is a necessity. This is Stage 2. Stage 2 is when the disease becomes very serious and certainly must be reviewed with the individual's Doctor. Generally, at this stage, the individual's Doctor might begin to give the individual some memory tests. I recommend that the individual not be told that they are being given the test, just have someone ask these general questions during a routine discussion or evaluation. I believe that if the individual is told of the test, there is a potential for the results to be skewed. Some answers given may be correct, but other simple ones, like the city where the individual resides may not be known. Some medicines may be prescribed after this testing. The individual will generally be aware that they are now forgetting some things.

Dementia – Alzheimer's next stages are now more serious and the individual should be in a situation where they can be adequately watched and with proper care, perhaps Care Givers or Family (nearly a full time job). At what I will refer to as Stage 3, there is a continuation of more and more memory loss. This will include calling visitors or Family members by the wrong name. One interesting thing about this stage is the situation where the individual may say things about people or things that they likely would not have said prior to this disease. Again, almost like they were given truth serum.

Dementia – Alzheimer's at Stage 4 is when it is obvious that something mentioned 5 minutes ago will be forgotten, however, details of perhaps forty years ago will be remembered. At times, a reference or question will come up about the individual's parents, as if they were still living. They will ask about people that have obviously passed away many years ago, or perhaps a residence or job that they may have had many years ago. At this stage, having the individual watch an old time movie or television show in black & white is generally soothing to them. Perhaps, they are more comfortable with black & white television (and watching "I Love Lucy"), because they can remember it being that way.

Not all things are soothing however. This is about the time when another aspect of the disease can start. It is referred to as the individual being a "sundowner". The "sundowner" scenario occurs when the sun goes down in the evening, and thus the light outside changes from light to dark. Being able to see the change to dark can be very unpleasant for the individual and they may get very anxious and upset. The solution here is to insure that the drapes or curtains are closed in the early evening, before sundown, so that this change from daytime to nighttime is not seen. Another issue that can have a significant effect on the individual (and care givers/family) suffering from Dementia – Alzheimer's disease is when experience a bout with UTI (Urinary Tract Infection). Not only does the individual have no way of explaining what is affecting them, but it even causes more significant anxiety and distress. The test for UTI adds additional discomfort (a urine sample, may require a catheter be inserted, and the individual has no idea why this is being done), all adding to the mental anguish that the individual is already experiencing.

Dementia – Alzheimer's at Stage 5 is noticed by talking with the individual and they are talking or referencing something that only they are aware of. It is like they are watching a video of the past. They may be aware of what they are seeing or what their brain is producing and they want you to understand and be part of what they are "seeing" or talking about. They may discuss working with someone or cooking something where they need to have your help. They may mention that they need to get going someplace to take care of this issue right away. This seems very real to them. Generally, in order to not upset the individual, it seems to be best to acknowledge what they are seeing or talking about, and (nicely) change the subject.

Dementia – Alzheimer's Stage 6 is more of a continuation of Stage 5, however, now the discussion of what they are seeing or talking about becomes just non-coherent talk. This non-coherent talk can last for some time and include many different thoughts and discussions of items that are difficult to determine just what they may be now referring to. At this stage, attempting to change the subject may not change what they are talking about (the video that only they see may 'effectively' still be playing in their mind).

It may be difficult to have them stop repeating this non-coherent talk and the situation that they are discussing.

Dementia – Alzheimer's Stage 7 requires nearly round the clock care from Care Givers, Retirement Home Staff, and/or Family. It is at this stage that even the most basic of life's functions are being forgotten, such as how to feed themselves with a fork. For almost everything they do now requires assistance. Clearly this is a dangerous situation where round the clock care is an important consideration by the Family.

Finally, at Stage 8, the Dementia – Alzheimer's disease, which has affected the brain and memory of the individual, appears to start shutting down systems of the body, as if the brain doesn't remember how these bodily systems function. Breathing and lung capacity may become reduced, perhaps requiring oxygen to sustain life. Internally, it is difficult to determine what other body parts or organs are affected, but the overall health is now in a steady decline, until the individual has unfortunately passed.

Dealing with the Good Times (which are few)

It is difficult to state that there are some positive aspects of the Dementia – Alzheimer's disease. It is fortunate that the individual is not aware of the advanced memory issues that they are experiencing, especially at the higher stages of the disease. They will not remember that yesterday, or even earlier today, that they had an issue with an illness or pain. If they have the unfortunate situation of having a spouse pass, they will not likely remember or know about that situation, and in order to spare them any bad feelings, it is believed it is best that they do not have the spouse's passing shared with them, or remembered or discussed, as there is no benefit of them knowing or thinking about that situation or any family member that may have passed (yet, they still ask about them), as this could only add to their overall distress, which still can happen, as noted by the "sundowner" episodes.

Remembering the Old Times

One of the amazing aspects of the Dementia – Alzheimer's disease is that the individual may recall instances, happenings and people from 40 or 50 years ago. They may ask about these people, perhaps their parents or other family in a way that indicates that these folks were just out and about yesterday. Again, it is like they see these folks in a "video" of their mind. However, mentioning something that happened two minutes ago is completely lost and not remembered.

Dealing with the Bad Times (most of the time)

As noted, this is a very cruel disease, and for Care Givers, Retirement Home Staff (or referred to as "Memory Care Staff") and Family as it requires a lot of patience and understanding; with the incoherent talk and discussions of something that only the Dementia – Alzheimer's patient is aware. At the latter stages of the disease, clearly the individual with the Dementia – Alzheimer's disease has no realization of what is happening to them. By this time they do not realize that they have lost their short term memory. The individual may exhibit anxiety and stress some days, and then feel fine the next day. There is no way to tell when they will have good days, and when they will have bad days.

Forgetting what just Happened

As noted, the crux of this disease is the loss of short term memory, and the incoherent talk that accompanies what the patient is "seeing" of this "video" that is playing only in their mind. Additionally, they may ask the same question over and over and over again, with the response forgotten almost as quickly as it is given. Again, this is the time (after the same multiple questions) where the subject should be changed to something/anything else (in a kind manner).

Coping

Again, this is difficult and hurtful for the family, who do not want to see and hear what the Dementia – Alzheimer's patient is going through, knowing the wonderful person that they used to know that was so full of life and able to live it to the fullest (yet, now they know that can no longer be the case). The individual with the Dementia – Alzheimer's disease, fortunately doesn't know what is happening to them, so they can cope pretty well until the later stages of the disease.

Documentation & Handling of Personal Affairs of the Patient

It is recommended that someone in the family of the patient that has Dementia-Alzeheimer's get the following formal authority as soon as possible:

1. Power of Attorney.
2. Become Trustee of Trusts & maintain a copy available at all times.

3. Become a Representative Payee when a parent/family member with Dementia/Alzheimer's can no longer handle their own affairs (or any elderly individual). This is critical for handling of monies, such as Social Security money that is received and used for the individual (where the Representative Payee is taking care of these monies). There is information on the Internet from Social Security on how to handle this situation. Additionally, all Social Security and Medicare Issues can be handled by the Representative Payee.

Help

There are many organizations where one can get information, support and questions answered including the Alzheimer's Association, the Mayo Clinic and the National Institute of Aging. It is not proven if Dementia-Alzheimer's is hereditary or not, but if there is a family history, there are more options to consider now in dealing with the mental health aspects. Discuss this situation early on with your doctor.

CHAPTER 21

QUALITY OF LIFE

As people age, the need for higher levels of care will increase. Even in the best circumstances, it is likely that there will be the need for additional time for Care Givers (Stage 3) and/or Family to support basic and now more extreme care. This will include (potentially) the need to have assistance with the routine, which may include bathing, toileting, or even dressing. With the loss of muscle tone, the additional level of care may include assistance getting in/out of bed or a chair. In more extreme circumstances, just getting out of any chair may require assistance, and now "lifts" are being used for this purpose. Generally, the lifts can be operated by a single Care Giver. Both the individual and the Care Giver need to be very careful with the lifts, such that a fall does not occur by accident. The Care Giver and Retirement Home Staff must be trained in the use of this equipment, in order to reduce the potential for accidents.

Of course, Falls have a higher probability of happening at any time. Due to existing health issues, or generally as people reach their 80's, they are fall risks. This is something that must be reviewed with the Care Givers and Retirement Home Staff. Any fall can be catastrophic.

With Dementia – Alzheimer's patients, an additional level of care is nearly a must for all the reasons mentioned previously, and the level of care increases as the stages of the disease progresses.

Physical immobility and reduced mental capacity will primarily dictate the amount of additional care and type of that care. Certainly a reduction in the mental capacity has a number of ramifications in care, from eating to the ability and consent to take medicines. At times the individual (for unknown reasons) may refuse, fight or not want to take their medicines (especially those individuals in the latter stages of Dementia – Alzheimer's). This can be very difficult for the Care Givers, Staff or Family. At times the medicines will need to be hidden in food, such as applesauce or ice cream (anything the individual may be willing to digest).

With the advancement in age, the need for assistance and support of Care Givers and Family grows. With more requirements for care, less mobility and less mental capacity, the quality of life becomes a concern. If they can no longer bathe themselves without help, are they happy? If they require help with toileting and need to wear adult diapers, and then perhaps make a mess relative to the diapers, are they really happy? If they can no longer get out of a chair or bed without assistance, are they enjoying life? If they can no longer feed themselves, are they enjoying life? If they have no memories, are they enjoying life? If they are in constant pain and anguish due to health issues, can they be enjoying life? What if they can no longer get out of bed? What if all the above is now the normal routine for them? These are the quality of life questions? The decision on the quality of life question is an issue for the Folks and the Family. Not making any judgments on this issue, but currently (according to Wikipedia) there are 6 states or areas in the country that allow some sort of legal euthanasia (recommended to verify your own state's legality & availability to perform):

> **Washington**, **Oregon**, **California**, **Vermont** and Bernalillo County, **New Mexico** [1]; its status is disputed in **Montana**.[11] Hopefully; the lack of quality of life does not result in going to this extreme step.

CHAPTER 22

HOSPICE

Many have heard about "Hospice", but not know how it works. Relative to the inevitably of passing, the final phase of Care Giving is Hospice. Hospice is generally called at the last stage of the individual's life. This is done when the individual (primarily via the Family or the Doctors) determine that the individual has about only 6 months or so prior to their passing. Hospice care is called upon not just for the elderly, but for any individual (due to an unfortunate illness or injury) that needs it.

"Hospice care is a type of care and philosophy of care that focuses on the palliation (def.: the relieving or soothing the symptoms of a disease or disorder without effecting a cure – <u>The American Heritage College Dictionary</u>) of a chronically ill, terminally ill or seriously ill patient's pain and symptoms, and attending to their emotional and spiritual needs. In Western society, the concept of Hospice has been evolving, starting in Europe in the 11th century. Then, and for centuries thereafter in the Roman Catholic tradition, hospices were places of hospitality for the sick, wounded, or dying, as well as those for travelers and pilgrims.

Within the United States, the term is largely defined by the practices of the Medicare system and other health insurance providers, which make hospice care available, either in an inpatient facility or at the patient's home, to patients with a terminal prognosis (by a doctor) who are medically certified to have less than six months to live.

Hospice in the United States has grown from a volunteer-led movement to improve care for people dying alone, isolated, or in hospitals, to a significant part of the health care system. In 2010, an estimated 1.581 million patients received services from hospice. Hospice is the only Medicare benefit that includes pharmaceuticals, medical equipment, twenty-four-hour/seven-day-a-week access to care, and support for the loved ones following a death. Hospice care is also covered by Medicaid and most private insurance plans. Most hospice care is delivered at the family home. Hospice care is also available to people in home-like hospice residences, nursing homes, assisted living facilities, veterans' facilities, hospitals and prisons.

Hospice plays an important role in reducing Medicare costs. Over the past 20-30 years, 27-30% of Medicare's total budget was spent on individuals in their last year of life. Hospice care reduces ER visits and impatient hospitalization which is costly and emotionally traumatizing for both the patient and their loved ones."[1]

Hospice personnel are specially trained to deal with this inevitably of the individual's passing. They are trained, often registered nurses that specialize in this care, and they visit the patient from time to time to see how things are progressing. The nurses make evaluations and provide important information to the family about what is happening and why. They are a great benefit, and their knowledge, understanding and the information they provide is very beneficial. They have a spirit of care and are able to play an important role in the final months and days of the individual's life. During the difficult and stressful times for the family, when the inevitably of passing occurs, Hospice provides quality of care, a sense of calm and caring professionalism, and expertise in a time of great emotion and sadness.

CHAPTER 23

PASSING WITH DIGNITY

Care Givers

Entering the last years of life, Care Givers (noted as Stage 3 for the Care Givers) play such an important role in assisting the Family with the elderly patients. If the primary Care Giver is now or has always been a family member, the same applies. Being understanding of a difficult situation is something that set Care Givers apart. Care at this stage means seeing the worst part of the evolution into old age and all the aspects associated with that. It takes a special person to be able to handle this, knowing that the inevitable will likely happen soon.

Medical Decisions/Advanced Directives

When reaching this highest required level of care, and having Hospice involved, the medical decisions now become more and more emotional. It is certainly hoped that all documentation of the individual's wishes are known per the Advance Directives' Documents. This does not make this time any easier, as there is still considerable emotion, but with the support of these documents, with the assistance of Hospice, the tough family decisions can be made.

Living Trusts

The Advanced Directives are part of the Living Trust Documents that were hopefully prepared legally a number of years ago. As these are emotional times already, the review and use of the Living Trusts help to ease an already difficult timing of the eventual passing, and it does so per their wishes.

Final Decisions

The Final Decisions should be done with confidence that it is the way that was desired, as spelled out in the Living Trust Documents. Having the plan for the passing, the way they wanted it to occur, gives some solace during a very difficult and emotional time.

Funeral Arrangements

Relative to passing, hopefully, the Funeral Arrangements have been pre-planned. It definitely reduces the emotional pain that the family is going through. It allows for more focus on their lives, not their passing.

This is an extremely difficult time for the family, and thus it is best if all the arrangements were pre-planned so that this occasion can go smoothly and efficiently, with the least amount of additional stress, in an already stressful period. Some of the items to think about (if pre-planned) are the important legal issues, decisions made in advance, burial or cremation plans and any special considerations.

Some of the recommendations made by the California Department of Consumer Affairs in 2010 where (a review of the states' legal arrangements should be made):

> "By asking the right questions, comparing prices and services, and making informed decisions, (you) one can make arrangements that are meaningful to your (one's) family and control the costs for yourself and your survivors (when pre-planning)."[2] Again, the key is pre-planning, which should save time, money and have the arrangements as desired.

> In California, the "law lists those who have the right, duty, responsibility to make decisions about disposition arrangements after a person's death. They are in order:

> - A person, prior to his or her death.
> - An agent under a power of attorney for health care.
> - The surviving competent spouse or the registered domestic partner.
> - The surviving competent adult child (often the Successor Trustee) or the majority of the surviving competent adult children.
> - The surviving competent parent or parents.
> - The surviving competent adult sibling or the majority of the surviving competent adult siblings.
> - The surviving competent adult person or the majority of the surviving competent adult persons, in the next degree of kinship.

A person may direct in writing the disposition of his or her remains and specify the funeral goods and services desired (often in the Living Trust Documents). Unless there is a written statement to the contrary that is signed and dated by the person, these directions may not be changed in any material way except as required by law."[2]

In California, the "law requires funeral establishments to quote prices over the telephone and to give you a General Price List (GPL) and a Casket Price List (CPL) when you inquire in person about arrangements and prices. (Also), the law allows a funeral establishment to set a fee for professional services, such as a funeral director's time spent:

- Helping you plan the funeral;
- Making arrangements with a cemetery or crematory (or other funeral establishment if the body will be shipped out of the area);
- Obtaining the death certificate (recommend that 8-12 copies are made) and other required permits(/documents);
- Submitting the obituary, and "unallocated overhead," which includes taxes, insurance, advertising, and other business expenses (recommended that this should be stated upfront, and thus understood up-front)."[2]

There are still many decisions to be made at this time, even when the ceremony has been pre-planned, including the determination of the actual date of the funeral (based on the availability of the burial location), arrangements for the casket or cremation vessel (if the cremated remains are to be scattered, where and how), flowers, obituary notifications, family notifications, governmental notifications (thus, the required numerous copies of the death certificate), and if the body is to be transported elsewhere (i.e. another state, perhaps airline arrangements), and of course, a religious clergy person (if so inclined) to preside over the funeral occasion.

CHAPTER 24

THE NEW AGE OF GROWING OLD

There are positive aspects and potential for happiness and fulfillment in the retirement years, for the elderly and their family, which may act as Care Givers for them. Proper planning and knowing about the necessary steps to take to deal with the financial and health issues will reduce the stress and anxiety of this stage of life. Taking the time to insure that all the documentation (Trusts, Wills, Directives) are in place will result in less emotional stress on the Family and improve overall quality of life for the elderly individuals. The knowledge gained from reading the proceeding chapters will benefit those beginning the journey of the retirement years; for the families and the Care Givers, with the potential for successful, continued quality of life in retirement.

Will we be ready for the retirement years? It does not appear that way. An article in the San Diego Union Tribune on May 20, 2016[13], noted that, "two-thirds of Americans reported that they would have difficulty coming up with the money to cover a $1,000 emergency. This was reported across all income levels". That doesn't make it seem like people will be ready for retirement in the new millennium. Who will take care of them? How will they afford the (multiple) thousands of dollars in costs, required monthly expenses in retirement? We could be facing a major economic crisis.

In the New Age of Growing Old, the health care issues and costs will play a significant role, thus pre-planning for this inevitability is crucial. Still there are many issues to resolve, monitor and consider by the elderly retirees and their families in order to make the retirement years as fulfilling as possible. The knowledge regarding what will occur, what is needed, what can happen, is extremely helpful and beneficial, thus the information has been provided in this book that covered a significant portion of these issues. I only wish our family had understood more of these issues and especially the best way to deal with them. Thus, as a reference guide to the important topics of this book, see the following Table; are you ready for these issues?

Reference Table of Key Issues for Retirement and Growing Old	Check-Off "X"
Decision on Moving from Family Home to Assisted Living or Retirement Facility	
Financial Planning with Financial Advisors - reviewing Savings/Investments	
Reverse Mortgage Evaluation, if available	
Decision on Maintaining/Driving a Vehicle	
Having Trusts/Wills/Health Care Directives Documents	
Review of Retirement Living Costs, @ Home or Retirement Facility	
Review of Retirement Living "add on" Costs	
Downsizing Home (Furniture, Personal Items) to a Retirement Facility	
Managing Medical Services, Prescriptions & Health Care	
Family managing Cash, Checkbooks, Jewelry, Family Heirlooms –secure them.	
Family managing Care Givers – monitor them	
Managing Illnesses of Age, i.e. Urinary Tract Infections(UTI), Shingles	
Dealing with "Change"	
Dealing with Mood Swings	
Dealing with "Falling" & not calling "911"	
Dealing with Hospitalization/Emergency Rooms – Documentation Pre-Planning	
Dealing with Medicare &Social Security (Annual Changes) & Health Insurance Plans – review for correctness	
Knowledge of Dementia – Alzeheimer's Disease	
Insuring Quality of Life Issues	
Knowledge of Hospice	
Passing with Dignity, per the individual's wishes/Funeral (Pre) Planning	

REFERENCES

1. "Hospice", Wikipedia, the free encyclopedia, http://en.wikipedia.org/wiki/Hospice.
2. "Consumer Guide to Funeral and Cemetery Purchases", California Department of Consumer Affairs Cemetery and Funeral Bureau, www.cfb.ca.gov, California Law of February 2010.
3. 'U.S. Department of Health and Human Services' Centers for Medicare & Medicaid Services', "Medicare & You 2016".
4. "Aetna Medicare Choice Plan PPO (2016), Y0001_1095_5494", Approved 08/2015, page 13.
5. "An Aging Nation: The Older Population in the United States", Current Population Report by Jennifer M. Ortman, Victoria A. Velkoff, and Howard Hogan, Issued May 2014, U.S. Department of Commerce, U. S. Census Bureau.
6. "Older Person's Health", CDC Centers for Disease Control and Protection, CDC 24/7: Saving Lives Protecting People™.
7. Alzheimer's Association, alz.org[R], http://www.alz.org/alzheimers_disease_1973.asp.
8. "What Really Causes Alzheimer's Disease", Well Being Journal, September/October 2015, Vol. 24, No. 5, Pages 10-15.
9. "Cost of Living in Retirement, "How to Figure out your Real Cost of Living in Retirement", Darrow Kirkpatrick, www.Money.com, July 16, 2014.

10. "Cost of Living in Retirement, "How to Figure out your Real Cost of Living in Retirement", Darrow Kirkpatrick, www. Money.com, July 16, 2014.
11. "Euthanasia", Wikipedia, the free encyclopedia, http:// en.wikipedia.org/wiki/Euthanasia.
12. "What are the Odds of Living to 100?", DiscoverTheOdds. Com, pages 1-10, December 14, 2013.
13. "Poll: $1K Crisis Tough for most in US", San Diego Union Tribune, Business Section C, Friday, May 20, 2016, Page C1.
14. "Discovering the True Cost of at Home Caregiving", NPR.org, 2012.

.

Printed in the United States
By Bookmasters